WHAT THE
UNITED
STATES
WANTS

WHAT THE

UNITED
STATES
WANTS

The **ESSENTIAL ROADMAP** for
International Candidates Applying
for **Study, Work,** and **Visa Opportunities**

JÚLIA KIRST, Ph.D.

What the United States Wants:
The Essential Roadmap for International Candidates Applying
for Study, Work and Visa Opportunities

For permissions, contact Júlia Kirst at contact@juliakirst.com.
For more information and bulk orders, or to learn about related
online trainings, speaking engagements, and services, visit
www.juliakirst.com.

Cover and Interior Design: David Provolo
Editing and Proofreading: Sophia Nelson

Library of Congress Control Number (LCCN): 2021923434

ISBN: 979-8-9852791-0-8 (print)
ISBN: 979-8-9852791-7-7 (e-book)

Published and printed in the United States

First Edition

For Anna Mae Patterson

TABLE OF CONTENTS

INTRODUCTION

When I arrived in the United States from Brazil a few decades ago, my first home in this then-foreign country was the Hospitality House. Through a series of extraordinary circumstances, I landed in Minnesota midwinter in what was supposed to be a short stay to improve my English.

It was at the Hospitality House that I began learning the ins and outs of this country, all with a most wonderful guide, Anna Mae Patterson, to whom this book is dedicated.

She was the one who patiently convinced me I should not wait for a bus to take me to my English classes in the minus 20-degree Fahrenheit weather because that kind of cold was dangerous. At first I resisted, for I was a 19-year-old keen on being independent. But when the kid from Saudi Arabia showed up to the first day of class with dark areas around his knuckles, I knew she wasn't kidding. The spots on my classmate's hands were frostbite! The skin damage had occurred the day before when he carried his suitcase—without gloves—for the short distance between the taxi and his dormitory entrance.[1] That moment was just the first of many times I had to admit I knew very little about the United States.

---

1 If you are coming to the northern parts of the United States from a tropical country and have a choice of when to come, make the transition during the American spring, summer, or fall. Avoid winter because, at this time of the year, the shock on body and mind is going to be intense. You are probably going to want to turn around and go home before the adventure even starts!

There were delightful surprises, too. Anna Mae's neighborhood had a diner, which I didn't know then is just another name for a small and simple American restaurant often located in a kind of trailer. There, I tried my first malted milkshake. I couldn't believe my tastebuds!

In Anna Mae's pantry, I discovered the first bag of tortilla chips of my life and ate it all in one sitting. As they say here, I thought I had died and gone to heaven! But I hadn't bought the chips myself, so I delighted in their taste and worried about where I would find more to replace the bag. Imagine my surprise when I discovered that this delicacy could be found just about anywhere food was sold!

Such unexpected delights are one of the great pleasures of traveling and venturing into new worlds, aren't they?

In those first days in the United States, I discovered that my English skills were less advanced than I had thought. (Isn't that so true for most of us?) And that put me in some funny situations, especially when I left the safety of Anna Mae's house and started to take English as a Second Language (ESL) classes at a local university.[2]

In my first few days in the ESL program, I brought my own lunch to class. After all, who knew how I would fare ordering food with my broken English? Near the end of

---

2 In those days, programs to learn English were still called English as a Second Language or ESL programs. This was because of the simplistic idea that people who were learning English were learning only their second language. All around the world—though not so much in the United States—people speak more than one language well before they begin to learn English. So, if you are looking for an English program in the U.S., choose one that describes itself as offering "English for Speakers of Other Languages" or ESOL, not ESL.

the first week of classes, I felt a bit more adventurous and went to the main road along the university campus to see if I could find something to eat. Everything was new, including the look of the buildings—which now sounds like a strange thing to say. I remember distinctly having a hard time identifying places and landmarks, as if my brain had to revise the very meaning of "landmark."

That early afternoon, as I wandered down the street near the campus, I spotted a sign on a window that said FOOD. Looked promising. There was another word in front of "food" but I paid little attention because I didn't know what it meant. I opened the restaurant's door with some nervousness: Would my English be good enough to order a sandwich? How would I manage all the questions they would inevitably ask about bread options, cheese options, and veggie options? I also felt mildly annoyed knowing that I would need to satiate my hunger with a measly sandwich. My Brazilian stomach was used to having a nice hot meal in the middle of the day.

I walked into what I thought was a restaurant and quickly learned the meaning of the word before "FOOD." PET FOOD! Enormous bags of dry cat and dog food covered the floor! Embarrassed, I turned around and headed out the door.

Language mistakes such as these are easy to spot and laugh about, if not at the time they happen, then in the future. In our family, thirty years later, we still laugh about the mistake made by my children's father, an American, when he came to Brazil for the first time. It was a hot day, and we stopped at a popsicle stand to refresh ourselves.

Trying out his newly acquired Portuguese skills, he asked for a cocô popsicle. All the Brazilians within earshot laughed heartily, while he wondered what had happened. Coco, with the stress on the first syllable, means coconut. That was, of course, the flavor he wanted. Instead, he asked for cocô. The word, when the last syllable is stressed, means excrement. Once he realized what had happened, he laughed with us, and all was well.

Unlike language slips, cultural mistakes are much harder to explain and laugh off. Misinterpretations about what is acceptable and unacceptable behavior can have negative consequences, sometimes with lasting effects. Imagine, for example, that you are a newcomer to a country and, when you meet someone for the first time, you reach to give that person a hug. Now, let's imagine that in this country this sort of intimacy is reserved for married couples. There won't be easy laughs in response. There will be discomfort, and possibly someone wondering about what you meant with that hug: "Did he just not know, or did he do it on purpose?" "How could she not have known?" "Did she just pretend she didn't know?" And so on and so forth.

———

This book is about those situations where cultural illiteracy is less funny and more consequential. More specifically, it is about situations when golden opportunities, such as a seat at a competitive university program or a dream job at a prestigious company, are at stake.

I wrote this book to help you understand the values that most of the people of the United States live by but would be hard-pressed to describe if asked. Learning about these values would normally just be a matter of curiosity. But for you, it is rather important knowledge to have.

> ▪ **When you apply for an opportunity to study, work, or get a visa in the United States, it is crucial to be able to tune into the sensibilities of the people who will assess your application. Without it, your hopes will remain unfulfilled dreams.**

This book was written to help you avoid missing opportunities in the United States simply because you didn't know how to meet unspoken expectations. It is based on real-life experiences reported to me by the many international students and professionals whom I have guided over the years.

Some of these professionals had missed exceptional opportunities before we began working together. It was heartbreaking to hear about their missteps, knowing that there is a simple solution: to reach for insider knowledge that can help you present your best self in a manner that is understood, respected, and valued by the gatekeepers to the opportunities you seek in the United States.

My goal with this book is to give you that insider knowledge and the tools to help you grow and thrive in the United States, no matter what country you come from. I am a firm believer that when people understand the value of this talent, everybody gains. I also believe that every person who wants to contribute should be worthy of a spot on this soil and under this sun. If this is you, read on!

I have been adjusting to American expectations for about 27 years. My first time living in the United States—the one that started at the Hospitality House—lasted nearly three years. I studied English first and then transferred my credits from a Brazilian university to Saint Olaf College in tiny Northfield, Minnesota, graduating two years later with a degree in Theater.

I have continued the work of adapting to the United States since 1997, the year of my second arrival. In the years since, I have had many opportunities to learn more about how things work in the United States and how to best respond to cultural expectations. I applied and was accepted to graduate programs at various universities. I attended Harvard for my master's degree and went to Brandeis for my Ph.D. Throughout my studies and after completing my Ph.D., I applied to and got jobs teaching at several colleges and universities. I also took non-academic jobs and did all the other things that often come with adopting a new country: buying a house, later buying another house and renting the former, seeking public and private schools for my children, going through the process of becoming a citizen, and running a couple of businesses of my own.

With each experience, I understood a little more. And because I am an anthropologist—a professional who is trained to see and understand culture—I was likely paying attention to what I was observing a little bit differently than most people would. In fact, when the time came to decide where I would do my dissertation research in cultural anthropology, I took the unusual step of not heading to an "exotic" country. As I told my professors in the doctoral program, the United States is my exotic country and I have been studying its people since my arrival.

In anthropology, there is a term used to describe a researcher who has become fully enmeshed in the community they are studying, to the point that they have become one of them. It is called "going native." What you will find in this book is what I learned in the process of "going native," so that you can get better at becoming a native yourself.

This book has two parts. "Part I: Values" contains eight chapters about big ideas such as "success" and "productivity." The core of these chapters is a description of the concept, accompanied by examples of how Americans use it in daily life.

Each chapter in the "Values" section also includes practical recommendations about how to apply the concept when preparing application materials. Some chapters in "Values" include additional questions to consider. These questions can help candidates feel more confident when they meet the people and situations that stand between them and the opportunity they want.

"Part II: Application Materials" has six chapters, each dedicated to a different type of document you are likely to need for your application. From transforming your resume into its American version to preparing for an interview, these chapters contain practical advice specifically developed for international candidates. This material is based on my studies, personal experiences, and the training and document-writing I have done for my clients over the years. Of course, you will need to adapt these instructions to your particular case, but these chapters provide a strong foundation.

> **Gatekeepers are the people who hold the keys to the metaphorical gates you hope will open for you. They have access to things and people that you want to reach. For example, an admissions officer or an interviewing professor are gatekeepers. A human resources director is a gatekeeper, as is an administrator with the power to get you (or not) an appointment with a busy company director.**

As you begin reading, you will find that many chapters are intertwined to some degree. For example, the chapter "Productivity" will also cover topics discussed in the chapter "Time." The chapter "Success" will also touch on ideas from the chapter "Individualism." Throughout the book, I note such cross-references so that, if you wish, you can examine this overlap with more ease.

Before we jump in, let's talk about a couple of matters of representation that deserve a little attention. "Matters of representation," in anthropological parlance, are considerations about how words do or do not reflect properly what they are meant to describe.

The first matter of representation I want to bring your

attention to is the habit of using the word "America" to describe the United States, and the term "Americans" to describe its people. A quick look at the world map reveals that America is a vast continent that includes South, Central, and North America. Using "America" to mean "the United States" is not just inaccurate but also ethnocentric (more on this in "Why Values Matter"). This use of the term "America" seems to imply that "we, the United States, are the ones who matter most in the Americas."[3]

Given this problem with the use of the word "America" to describe a country, I have aimed to use "United States" instead of "America" throughout the book. I have also tried to use "the people of the United States" instead of "Americans" whenever possible. But at times, I do use the less accurate terms because doing differently would sound awkward in the sentence structure. So, if you come across "America" or "Americans" in this book, remember that these terms were selected for convenience only. There is nothing geographically or historically accurate about calling this part of the world "America" and its people "Americans." (It goes without saying that if we were to use the term "Americans" accurately, we would be referring exclusively to the indigenous people of the continent.)

The second matter of representation refers to the expression "the values of the United States." This choice of words can give the impression that the people of this country are one big collective that shares most, if not all, values. This

---

3 Perhaps the ownership of "America" and "Americans" is not contested because the United States is quite literally on top of the world. Something similar used to happen with the term "men." We used to say "men," as in "the history of men," when we meant "men and women" or "humanity."

could not be further from the truth. Not only are the dimensions of the country gigantic, making for a wide range of geographic, political, social, and economic experiences, but the United States is also, quite literally, made of a world of different people and groups holding different beliefs and hopes for the future, and often interacting and creating amalgamated perspectives as they go.

When I write about "what the United States values," I am not asserting that there is a single set of values guiding the day-to-day of all people in the country. I am saying, however, that despite the diversity of people and perspectives represented in this country, there is a consensus in professional circles about what constitutes success and what is a person with or without the potential to succeed. As much as the country contains plenty of diverse perspectives, there is a general agreement about who is a "promising" candidate. This consensus is what I describe in the coming pages because this is what matters most to international applicants.

———————

This book will interest anybody who wants to understand more about what the United States values. In other words, it can be simply a text that satisfies the curious mind.

But for those who grew up in countries other than the United States and are preparing an application for an opportunity here, this text is not just a curiosity, but an essential roadmap.

Those most likely to profit from the guidance in this book include:

International professionals who are

- working toward the revalidation of their credentials in the U.S.
- seeking additional training or other forms of professional advancement in the U.S.

Immigrants who are

- looking to obtain employment-based U.S. immigrant and non-immigrant visas.

International students seeking a spot in

- undergraduate programs in colleges and universities in the U.S.
- graduate programs in colleges and universities in the U.S.

International business leaders who are

- working in partnership with an American company.
- working for a U.S. company.

A better understanding of what the United States wants and values will help you achieve not just the opportunity you seek now. It will also support your success once you have walked through the open gates to the opportunity that brought you to this country in the first place. That is to say, the adventure we are starting here will serve you for life.

I couldn't be more excited for you and want to thank you for allowing me to be part of your journey!

Júlia Kirst, Ph.D.

PART 1:
VALUES

1

WHY VALUES MATTER

Imagine that you have a crush on someone. You desperately want to be with this person. You feel in your gut that you will be happier with this person by your side, even if you don't yet know everything there is to know about them.

Now, let's add to the mix: You don't speak this person's language very well and this person does not speak your language at all. You don't know the person's culture much, except for what you have seen in brief vacations to their country and in movies. And yet you are absolutely certain that this is the person for you.

You want to impress them—actually, more than that, you want them to love you! But how? What is the best way to make sure that they understand that you think of them as more than a friend? If you were preparing for a date, should you bring them flowers, chocolates, or just yourself at this stage of the game? If you decide to get flowers, should they be a simple bouquet of wildflowers? Or an impressive dozen of red roses? Could red roses have the opposite effect and repel your crush because it would be too much too soon? With so many unknowns and so much at stake, how can you be sure you are creating the right impression?

Trying to stand out among a crowd of applicants in the

United States when you are from another country is sort of like that. Even if you speak the language perfectly, there is a great deal you still don't know. You can only get to a "yes, come join us," if you present yourself, your accomplishments, and your potential in a way that can be understood, respected, and valued.

When we are dealing with culture, we have entered a realm of complex hidden rules and unspoken expectations that is difficult even for locals to explain. They can't describe it because our culture is so deeply part of who we are that we typically don't even see that it is there. American anthropologist Edward Hall was the first to use the analogy of an iceberg to explain culture. That was in 1976 and we still use this analogy because it makes sense.

Let's take a look.

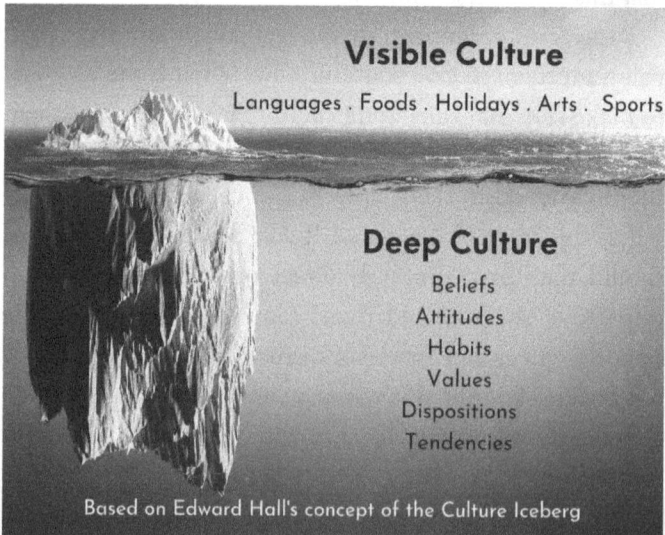

Visible Culture
Languages . Foods . Holidays . Arts . Sports

Deep Culture
Beliefs
Attitudes
Habits
Values
Dispositions
Tendencies

Based on Edward Hall's concept of the Culture Iceberg

The Culture Iceberg, like any iceberg, has a part that is above the water—the things we can see and articulate, such as "In this country we drive on the right side of the road, unlike places like England, where they drive on the left side of the road."

But below the visible tip of the iceberg, there is much more: the things that we have difficulty noticing and articulating to others and even to ourselves. Deep Culture is so much a part of us that if an outsider pointed out that our culture had an unusual belief or attitude, we might even get angry and say, "That's not about our culture! That is just normal!"

The underlying sentiment about Deep Culture is that these dispositions, values, attitudes, and beliefs are the norm; they are attitudes that anybody in their right mind would and should have.

This way of thinking is called Ethnocentrism. The term refers to the idea that other people's values are correct (or not) depending on how much they align with our own. Ethnocentrism is the very human habit of understanding others through the lens of what we consider the norm.

It is important to note that ethnocentrism is not a harmless misconception: it is often used as justification for treating those with values different from our own as less-than-human. Colonialism and the domination of the native people of the Americas were very much fueled by ethnocentric beliefs held by Europeans about the superiority of their ways.

Another way to think about Deep Culture is to think of it as the air we breathe, or, as David Foster Wallace wrote so eloquently, the water in which fish swim. In a now famous commencement address, the late Wallace told this story:

"There are these two young fish swimming along and they happen to meet an older fish swimming the other way, who nods at them and says 'Morning, boys. How's the water?'" And the two young fish swim on for a bit, and then eventually one of them looks over at the other and goes, 'What the hell is water?" Like air for us—and water for fish—culture is so ubiquitous that we don't even notice it is there. Should someone ask us questions about our Deep Culture, we would likely be puzzled.

I am an anthropologist, so I have been trained to see, think about, and articulate thoughts about culture. But if the term "culture" doesn't work for you, you can also think about it as "the values" a group of people cherishes (or abhors). Every community, small or large, has a collection of values that impacts what this group considers "good," "bad," "beautiful," "ugly," "virtuous," "shameful," and so on.

One of my favorite definitions of culture comes from John Omodhundro, in the book *Thinking Like an Anthropologist*. He writes: "The way people dress their babies, name the colors in the spectrum, torture their enemies, pay for bananas and acquire their leaders are a few of the human activities influenced by culture." I find this quote so profound because it shows that just about anything we do is affected by culture.

> Human beings are born and raised to view the world according to the ways of our particular people. We then grow up believing that our ways are simply how people do things everywhere.

If we never travel outside what is familiar to us, it is very normal to believe that our ways are universal. But if we travel, or if we simply pay attention to what people in different places say and do, we can see how much of what we thought was universal is uniquely ours. For example, among some religious communities, a man shows his devotion to God by letting his facial hair grow. In other religious communities, the exact opposite is true: a clean-shaven face is the most fervent sign of devotion to God. Same goal, opposite actions! One young man was taught to let his beard grow to honor God and the other young man was taught to shave often to honor God. Neither is wrong. They are simply different.

It is when we leave "home," usually quite literally, that we begin to learn that our values are not universal. Many years ago, when my kids were in daycare, they had a friend whose parents had taught him that broccoli was dessert. And so in his home he ate broccoli at the end of the meal, with the delight of someone eating dessert. One day, this child came to our house to play, and we invited him to stay over for dinner. He did, and when his mom came to pick him up, the boy told her with delight: "We had broccoli for dinner! Can we have dessert for dinner at our house too?" The child's understanding of what was dinner and what was dessert was rocked simply by leaving his home for a few hours.

Now magnify this experience by a hundred when you travel to a foreign country, particularly a country where you don't speak the language very well. Magnify this experience by a thousand when you not only visit a new place but also become a resident long-term.

Being exposed to other ways of doing things can be disconcerting. But it is also exciting and enlightening. This is why we say that international travel promotes cross-cultural understanding. It makes us more flexible in our thinking because we realize that "the way things are done" is just our way things are done. Fascinating, isn't it?

2

SUCCESS

THE CONCEPT

If you want to come across as a strong candidate in the United States, you must have a solid understanding of what the people reading your application consider "success." What will they be looking for? How can you show what you have to offer in a manner that they will recognize, respect, and desire to have in their organization? In this chapter, we go deeper into these questions.

But first, let's correct the common misconception that an application is mostly about proving that you can succeed in the future. The gatekeepers assessing your application will want to see much broader evidence of success across time.

They want to see a history of past successes. This shows that single instances of success were not a fluke, but part of a pattern. Such history is evidence that you are likely to succeed again.

They want to see signs of current success because this shows that you have remained committed to growth. It demonstrates sustained drive and stamina.

They want to see signs that you are likely to succeed in the future. Can you already see yourself as part of the team and are you able to articulate how you are going to contribute?

To illustrate these three points in time, let's look at concrete application examples.

Say you are applying to a college or university program in the United States. You will need to deliver past school records for a snapshot of your past successes. Admissions officers will also be interested in signs that you are succeeding now, as evidenced by records such as your current Grade Point Average (GPA) and your class ranking.[4] Last, admissions officers will look for signs that you have the potential to succeed in the future. This is a concern not just because they want you to succeed as a student in their program, but also because, after graduating, you will become a representative of their institution for the entire world to see.

This matter of who you become in the future, after you have graduated and become an alum of an American educational institution, is more important than most people realize. In the United States, when you graduate from a college or university, that institution's name becomes forever attached to your name. (This is also why people will spend a great deal of money for a five-day training at institutions like Harvard University. The student can then attach the renowned university's name to their own credentials, even if they have no actual degree from the institution.[5] Universities

---

4 Americans love rankings, so even if you don't have official numbers, there is typically a place in an application to explain in narrative form that calculating GPAs is not common practice in your country. In this section you can offer alternative indicators, such as the ranking of your university and your program.
5 For the record, a certificate for a five-day training is not a degree.

know they are attractive in this manner and offer these short courses at a hefty price because it is easy money.)

The link between student and educational institution is so significant that when you get a diploma from a high school, college, or university, that institution becomes your "alma mater," which is Latin for "nourishing mother." The attachment between institution and student for life couldn't be more explicit!

When you succeed post-graduation, your alma mater looks good too. For example, I was a faculty member at a college that took great pride in being an alma mater of the famed journalist Ronan Farrow, son of Mia Farrow. Similarly, when Hillary Clinton became the Democratic presidential candidate, her alma mater, Wellesley College, received a lot of attention from the national media and the public.

More attention means more student applications, which makes the institution more competitive to get into. The more competitive an institution, the more respect it gets in the academic market. This edge can greatly benefit the institution's finances.

A student's likelihood to succeed post-graduation is also a factor when an educational institution decides who receives financial aid. Giving generous aid to a promising candidate may be a small investment if a student is likely to benefit the institution's reputation in the future.

If you are applying for a job in the United States, your materials will be assessed for evidence of past successes, since your past is, at least in theory, an indicator of your potential to succeed in the future.

Because businesses are typically seeking new employees to multiply their own resources, your resume should clearly show:

- that you have a solid and consistent track record of multiplying resources for prior employers.
- that you can quickly step up and begin adding value for the employer, without requiring an unreasonable amount of their resources to get you ready to produce the benefits the employer seeks.

Your goal should be to demonstrate your past successes and your potential to hit the ground running to create more of what the company wants as quickly as possible. This is America's definition of a successful hire.

If you are applying for an immigration visa based on your qualifications (such as the EB2–National Interest Waiver), you will also be assessed by your record of successes in the past and present, and your promise to create value for the United States once you have been granted the visa.

Regarding the EB2-NIW visa, I cannot stress enough the importance of demonstrating that you can create value for the country. Too often, my clients tell me that they hope the United States Citizenship and Immigration Services (USCIS) will grant them a Green Card because they are dedicated and hardworking. While this quality is wonderful and may cause a good impression on the immigration officer assessing your documents, in general, immigration authorities in the U.S. do not care about your personal work habits. What they care about is whether you will create value for the country.

As we will see in more detail later, the United States is a country that runs on cost-benefit calculations and return on investment analysis. Like an employer looking for what value you can bring to a business, immigration authorities are assessing what value you can bring to the country. And that value must be demonstrated not in generic assertions, such as, "I believe I can really help the country," but in specific and verifiable statements based on how your skills fill a need.

> **Whether you are applying to a college or university, to a job, or for an immigration visa, never discuss how much you (or worse, your family) wish to move to the United States. The people assessing your application are not in the business of making you happy. Their role is to make themselves better because you joined them. Make it your goal to make clear how you can do that.**

An example would be, "I am prepared to bring my dentistry skills to areas of the United States identified as Dental Health Profession Shortage Areas (HPSAs) by the U.S. Health Resources & Services Administration." Notice that this example not only uses data (areas identified as HPSAs), but the data cited comes from credible and verifiable sources from inside the United States—in this case, the U.S. Health Resources & Services Administration. Other examples of useful sources include government agencies such as the U.S. Bureau of Labor Statistics for most professions (www.bls.gov), the Centers for Disease Control and Prevention for applications in the healthcare sector (www.cdc.gov), and the Federal Aviation for pilots (www.faa.gov), to name just a few examples. The focus of your application should always be on the value you are ready to bring to the country in a specific area of need identified by official agencies.

———

What, then, are the signs of a person who brings value to an educational institution, an employer, or the country? Let's look at some major indicators.

1. A person who is successful has goals. In the United States, the setting and having of goals has almost magical properties. A person with goals can see clearly where they are, where they are going, and why. Goals are perceived as providing more than direction: they create energy and give meaning to the goal-setter's life. Some even claim that their drive to reach goals keeps them young.

If life were a basketball game, having goals would be like being on the court playing and scoring. Not having goals would be like sitting on the bench hoping to get called some-day. While the person on the bench waited and hoped for an opportunity, the person on the court was already playing and actively creating their next opportunity to shine.

The movement toward the next and better goal is a value held dear by many Americans (see chapter "Progress"). Therefore, people who don't have goals, or who say they have them but are unable to do what it takes to reach them, are seen as lacking ambition.

Sitting back and watching life pass you by would be a waste of potential, especially in a country that prides itself on being the land of opportunity. Not having goals would be a dreadful demonstration of the inability to "seize the day." (Remember the popularity of *carpe diem*?)

The opposite of sitting idly is to "grab life by the horns." This concept is so valued in the United States that it is the tagline for the all-American brand of cars and trucks, Dodge. And you can be certain that a phrase used in advertising for a major American brand points to a value that is widely shared by the culture.

Dodge is a registered trademark of FCA U.S. LLC.
Image used with permission.

2. A person who is successful is focused, persistent, and ambitious. Having goals is important to Americans, but some goals are better than others. Goals worth embracing should be difficult to achieve. In fact, the greater the sacrifices required for achieving a goal, the more you are signaling that you have the spirit of a winner. Americans see obstacles as opportunities to test their determination. The idea is that a person who can overcome hurdles once is probably capable of overcoming hurdles in the future, too.

Besides testing one's commitment, big goals also present a chance to demonstrate and practice discipline. Many

Americans like to engage in what is called "reverse engineering," to determine what steps must be taken to reach a goal that is far in the future. In this technique, a person sets a future goal and then establishes the steps to get there, starting with the step furthest away from the present moment, but closest to the goal, and working backward toward the current position—the starting point. Moving forward consistently, with discipline, should lead the person to the result they seek.

> "No one ever got to the top of a mountain in one giant jump. Challenges can be overcome, and goals can be reached, but it can only happen one step at a time."
> — Doe Zantamata

3. A person who is successful is constantly improving. One pillar of American culture is the notion that everything in life is on a path toward improvement (see chapter "Progress"). In this perspective, winners pursue growth opportunities, while losers shy away from such opportunities and instead stay passively in their comfort zone. People destined to succeed are those who:

- find their power, moving from weakness to strength, both physically and mentally.
- find their voice, moving from silence to confidence and self-affirmation.
- find their wisdom, moving from confusion to focus and maturity.

- become more productive (learn a shortcut), more skilled (take a class), more generous (go volunteer), thinner (go on a diet), healthier (go on a different diet), and so on.

In this context, lack of success is believed to occur for one reason and one reason only: a personal failure to harness opportunities and overcome obstacles.

> "You yourself are your own obstacle.
> Rise above yourself."
> — Hafez

4. A person who is successful is the master of their own life. In the United States, success is a quality associated with individuals, not collectives (see chapter "Individualism"). People may say that a sports team was successful in a game or a season, yet news reporting about a team's win will often focus on individual stars. (Neighborhoods, towns, and other types of communities are rarely described as successful, even though it seems quite possible to imagine what a successful neighborhood or town would look like.)

"Success" is typically understood to be a quality of individuals who have leadership skills. Being a leader means you are at the helm of something because you have something to offer that others don't.

Americans believe that leadership qualities can be learned. Therefore, there is really no valid excuse to not be a leader. There is, in fact, a certain disdain for those who are content being followers. Jack Canfield, the author of Success

Principles and a motivational speaker with a large follow-ing in the U.S., is an example of this philosophy. One of his more popular quotes states that "People who don't have goals work for people who do."

We seem to forget that for someone to be a leader, oth-ers have to be followers. That's just how the math works and not a comment on a follower's character. Moreover, people have different strengths, and being the worker bee who exe-cutes the plan designed by a leader is not a sign of weakness, but simply a different kind of contribution. However, this would be a collective view of success, which is not the pri-mary way "success" is conceived in the United States.

PRACTICAL APPLICATIONS

1. When presenting your interest in an opportunity, explain it in the context of larger goals you have for your career. You become a stronger candidate when you can articulate how the opportunity in front of you is part of a journey toward something larger and admirable. For example, say you are applying for an internship with a famous cancer researcher. Explain your desire to join her cancer research lab as part of a larger wish to learn and hopefully help find the cure for cancer someday. If you can show that you are on a path toward something larger, and that the institution could become a part of that accomplishment in the future, you become more interesting than the candidate who does not articulate a future vision.

2. When discussing goals, state professional goals only. Do not explain your desire to join a program or company because of what this opportunity can bring to you personally. Nobody is interested in hearing about how much you and your family have dreamed of moving to the United States. These are considered personal matters. Though most immigrants do come to this country in pursuit of a better future for themselves and their families, this motivation should be left out of your application and interview.

3. You are a more attractive candidate when you can show that you have overcome obstacles to reach your goals. Think about challenges that depict you as someone determined to overcome anything that gets in your way. Describe how overcoming the challenge made you a better person. I cannot overstate Americans' fascination with stories about adversity serving as a springboard for success.

4. Remember that whether you are applying for an educational program, a job, or an immigration visa, those assessing your application want to know how you can help them succeed. Research information about the institution's goals and be prepared to show evidence that what they want is exactly what you can offer. The fit should look natural and undeniable.

ALSO THINK ABOUT THIS...

- What do you see yourself doing two, five, and ten years from now? If you don't have a vision for your long-term professional development, begin to create one. Whether or not you are asked about it directly, you must come across as someone who has a vision for your future.

3

PROGRESS

THE CONCEPT

Among modern nations, some are young, some middle-aged, and others historically mature. The United States is not a young child, but neither is it a full-grown adult. The country is rather like a teenager who is eager to and not entirely comfortable with transitioning into adulthood. Like many adolescents, the United States cares greatly about its image, especially how it compares with its peers. Not surprisingly, it is seduced by countries that boost its ego and dislikes countries that overtly disapprove of it. Like insecure youth, the country often engages in grandiose external actions and, at the same time, disregards the consequences of these actions on its own soil and abroad. At least for the time being, the United States lacks the serenity and self-assurance that comes with maturity.

In a country with so much to prove to itself and others, it is no wonder that many of its people are dragged into an endless search for ways of becoming more and better. Often unaware of it, we are constantly working to become you-take-your-pick: wealthier, healthier, thinner, smarter, calmer, more productive, more liked on social media, and so on. While aiming to improve as a person is obviously good for us, the notion that our value as human beings is directly tied to our ability to progress can get downright exhausting.

The eternal journey toward becoming "new and improved" is part of what it means to be an American. Because progress is so foundational, it is important to understand this concept when seeking to become part of the United States. After all, when you become a candidate for anything, you will be assessed on your ability to advance from where you are now to something much greater, along the way making those associated with you—your university, your company—greater as well.

Progress means, very simply, that today you are an improved version of who you were in the past.

The quintessential example of progress in the psyche of the United States is what is called the American Dream. The Merriam-Webster dictionary describes the American Dream as "a happy way of living that is thought of by many Americans as something that can be achieved by anyone in the U.S. especially by working hard and becoming successful."

What does that look like in practice? Here are just a few examples:

If today all you can afford is renting a room, in the future you should want and be able to rent an apartment; next in the sequence would come ownership of what is called a "starter house," perhaps a cheap construction in a neighborhood of dubious reputation; eventually, you should be able to afford a larger house in a great neighborhood, with a yard full of potential for weekend projects, including entertaining guests, who then would admire the story of where you came from and where you ended up through determination and sweat.

If today you use public transportation, the next step in the ladder of progress would be to save up and buy a small used car. This car would be parked on the street. As you improved your lot in life, you could afford a newer car and park it in a garage off the street. Ideally, your accomplishments would continue to propel you forward, and eventually you would reach car-heaven: your own shiny BMW parked in the large garage of your large new house!

Perhaps your first job paid you by the hour and had no perks. Then things improved, and you got a new job with benefits that included a week of paid vacation. Still early in your career, with little disposable income, you went camping in state parks for your too-short summer break. Then you progressed to two weeks of paid vacation and took that time off in a rented cabin with a kitchen, so you could make your own meals and avoid the cost of eating out. As you became more successful and had more disposable income, you started taking your family on cruises. Eventually, you could take the family on international vacations to beautiful places and stay at wonderful hotels a couple of times a year.

The American Dream also posits that progress is generational; that is, we are better off than our parents, our children will be better off than we are, and so on, in a never ending pattern of improvement.

The notion that if we embrace opportunities and use them wisely, we can achieve the success that was out of reach for our parents is appealing and the source of storylines for many popular fictional books and movies. But this is simply a concept—a nice idea. It does not reflect the fact that our progress is embedded in social, economic, and political systems that have clear preferences for some demographic groups over others. It also does not account for worldwide disasters such as the climate crisis and the COVID-19 pandemic; we haven't even started to understand the impact of these tragedies on our (in)ability to improve on the lot of our parents and their parents.

———————

For Americans, progress is desirable but not at all a natural state of affairs. Progress does not occur on its own, but must be worked toward, through the intentional establishment of goals and steps to reach them. (See chapter "Success.")

Goals can come in a variety of flavors:

A personal goal is the kind that improves some aspect of who you are. You may improve your wardrobe, your hair, your teeth; you may become better at falling asleep and staying asleep, at handling money, or at managing the day-to-day of a complex household. If this all sounds eerily familiar, it is because personal progress is the engine that moves social media.

A professional goal may include getting a job at a more prestigious firm than the one you work for at the moment, getting a promotion or a raise, increasing the number of people you supervise, increasing the company's revenue, or decreasing client complaints, to name just a few examples.

A consumer goal may be acquiring a newer and more advanced version of a computer, cell phone, or car.

An educational goal may be getting into a prestigious program, working with the most renowned professor in the program, getting published in the highest-ranking journals, or maybe earning a degree in record time.

Whatever the type of goal, promising candidates need to have at least one. Without goals, progress is virtually impossible!

—————

Progress is a movement to the top—as illustrated below—and in a straight line. Ideally, a person will move from point A to point B in a clear and uninterrupted manner.

However, as they say, "shit happens": accidents, illnesses, unexpected bills, and bankruptcy happen; divorce happens and swindlers happen; addiction happens, and so do earthquakes and wildfires. Slacking and inefficient use of time happen. The image below is a more accurate reflection of reality for most of us.

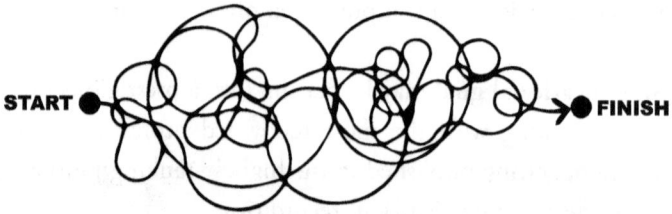

What are we to do with these setbacks that are more or less part of everybody's lives, without jeopardizing the progress narrative that is so valued in the United States?

You have probably heard the expression, "What doesn't kill you makes you stronger." In your narrative, you can and should talk about setbacks. This is particularly important if the setbacks caused gaps in your professional history, which may be all too clear in your resume. It is best to be proactive and examine how you can change your setback into a story about your ability to grow through adversity.

A good setback narrative can serve you in multiple ways besides providing a proactive explanation for a gap in your resume. In the chapter "Success," we talked about the value Americans place on character traits such as drive and persistence. Your setback narrative serves you best when it is presented as an obstacle that tested and reinforced these traits.

Let me present a metaphor. Think of yourself riding a horse. The horse represents your life, and you are in control of it. Then something unexpected happens, perhaps a thunderbolt, and, through no fault of your own, you are thrown off the horse. Now comes the test. Are you or aren't you going to get back on the saddle? Do you have what it takes to get back on it, like a true hero on a hero's journey? (See chapter "Personal Branding.")

A good setback narrative tells the listener not only about how you got back on the saddle—always through your own effort. (See chapter "Individualism.") It also:

- transforms a story that could have been interpreted as a disruption of the progress narrative into an organic part of it.
- shows your ability to pass difficult tests life may throw at you: it didn't kill you but made you stronger.
- presents an opportunity to show that you are the hero of your life, as opposed to someone at the mercy of what happens to you.
- allows you to show that you are exceptionally prepared to tackle unexpected obstacles in the future, when you have joined the organization that is assessing your application.

In this challenge-to-progress narrative, setbacks are not random or meaningless occurrences. Instead, they have a purpose: they came to teach you to persist and strengthen your vision.

Hardships often prepare ordinary people for an extraordinary destiny.
— C. S. Lewis

Since setbacks can serve a progress narrative, you can and should reveal whatever tried to hold you back. As long as you can transform gaps into stories of growth and movement toward something better, you will be fine.

PRACTICAL APPLICATIONS

1. Because the people assessing you are looking for signs of progress, you should present your most recent successes first. This is the reason a resume should always list your most recent position or accomplishment first. Ideally, your most recent position is more prestigious than the previous one, which is more prestigious than the one before, and so on.

   If your professional progress is not immediately apparent, there are other ways to encourage the reader to perceive evolution. For example, perhaps the title of your current position and your previous position is the same, but you are now at a more prestigious company. In such a case, list companies rather than positions first in each entry of the work history section of your resume.

2. Your application materials should contain plenty of evidence that you have continued to seek opportunities to grow professionally even after you completed the degrees and certificates required to practice your profession. As we have seen, in the United States you are expected to be continually moving toward something better and to never be satisfied with what you already have.

3. While you want to present yourself as having goals, you also want to show that you are open to growing in new directions. Flexibility is essential in today's job market and showing that you are willing to serve a company in any way that they see fit will be to your benefit. If you are applying for an educational program, it is even more important to present yourself as someone who is directed and also humble and ready to learn.

4. It is common for interviews to include questions about the candidate's strengths and weaknesses, and you may be wondering about how to answer the latter. A client recently asked me if stating that they are a perfectionist would be a good answer. It is not, and here is why: this answer so blatantly skirts the weakness question that it is almost embarrassing. Instead, you should present an issue that is a genuine challenge for you. This would not just be honest but would demonstrate self-awareness—two desirable traits in a candidate.

   For a convincing progress narrative, it is also desirable that, after identifying this weakness, you worked to overcome it. You can mention how you accomplished this and also state that you don't consider the work done because "there is always room to improve." In this manner, you will be presenting yourself as a person who is self-aware and proactive. Such an answer allows you to be honest and maintain the progress narrative at the same time.

ALSO THINK ABOUT THIS...

- What kinds of events have happened in your life and career that show progress? Are these events incorporated in your application materials, or do you need to review them to make sure your trajectory is one of undeniable evolution?
- Have there been significant setbacks in your professional development, and can you use them to show your ability to overcome obstacles and continue to progress despite them? For example, I had a client who suffered a life-threatening accident in his second year of college. The doctors told him that his memory was affected so badly that, if he wanted to go back to college, he would need to choose an easier major. He made the shift recommended by his doctors, but eventually felt that his first choice of profession was his real calling. He returned to his initial field and became highly successful. We used this story in his purpose statement to describe his passion for his original field and his drive to succeed in it, no matter what. You don't need to have survived a life-threatening accident to show your drive to persist and progress in your profession. But you probably have setback stories that are waiting to be told for a similar purpose. Use them!

4
TIME

THE CONCEPT

A few years ago, my parents were visiting me in the U.S., and we planned a trip to go see friends who live two hours away. We had been invited for 3 p.m. and, having been in the United States long enough, I knew to plan the two-hour drive so that we would arrive at my friends' house on the dot. When we were getting close to their home, my father looked at his watch nervously. It was one minute before 3 p.m.! He then asked me to drive around the block a few times so we wouldn't arrive at their door at exactly 3 p.m. because "they won't be ready for us!" From his cultural perspective, arriving on the dot rather than being a bit late would be rude.

In the United States, the end time of a visit is also often prescribed and followed. It wasn't until I came to this country that I saw an invitation with a starting time and an ending time! And this wasn't a child's birthday party, where an ending time may be needed so parents know when to pick up their little party-goers. It was an adult gathering in the yard of a professor's home. We were sitting outside on a beautiful summer evening having interesting conversations. All of a sudden, the professor stood up. I looked at my watch and saw it was exactly 6 pm, the time listed in the invitation as the party ending time. He had stood up to signal that the party was over!

Over time, such experiences became less personal. It is not that the professor didn't like us (necessarily). It is just that, in a culture where time is a precious commodity, these resources must be carefully allotted to different purposes and not just flow freely and aimlessly.

———————

Take a moment to think about what comes to mind when you imagine someone saying, "I don't have time now," or, "I won't have time to get together this month at all. I have been so busy, sorry." What assumptions come to mind about this person? Keep that in the back of your mind.

Now picture the opposite: someone says to you, "I don't know what to do with my time," or "I can see you anytime, my schedule is wide open." What assumptions come to mind about that person?

In the United States, these two scenarios typically conjure opposite assessments about the qualities of the speaker. The busy person is usually associated with positive characteristics: they are dedicated and committed, they have a vision for their future, and they work hard to reach their goals. That explains why they don't have time for smaller pleasures in life, like having a cup of coffee with you. It is excused.

If this very busy person were to take time off, it would probably be a nice vacation—not a cup of coffee with you. This is because hard work is supposed to result in deserved time off. "You are going on vacation? Good for you! You have been working so hard, you deserve it!" If the busy person replies that they are going on a vacation because their family or their doctor insisted that they take a break, but that they will need to take work with them, there will likely be admiration. Apparently, work can't go on without their input. Being "indispensable" has a nice ring to it, doesn't it?

On the other hand, the person who is free to go out for coffee at any day and time is much more likely to be perceived in a negative light. In the eyes of many Americans, this person may not be working hard enough toward their goals. Even worse, they may be lacking goals altogether and the drive to make something of their lives. And that would not only be unproductive but also indicate some weakness of character.

An older person with time on their hands is one thing—it is assumed one has paid their productivity dues to society. But a young person is supposed to be engaged in reaching total productivity as soon as humanly possible. Rather than "waste time," such a person is supposed to take ownership of their life and their future. (Remember the admonition to "Take Life by the Horns" from Dodge in the chapter "Success"?)

Whether in a job or a side hustle, a person shows their ability to progress and reach success by having little time available for activities unrelated to work. This was the thought behind a feature included in the scheduling software Acuity. The "Make Me Look Busy" feature is described on the company site as beneficial because it will "make you look like you're in high demand," even if you are not.

———

In this context, time is much more than simply a tool to help people get together at the same moment. Instead, time is a resource that can be used well or wasted. This resource, though technically abstract, is a commodity, so much so that we often hear that "time is money." We can "waste time," "spend it well," "manage it," and even "budget it"!

This inspirational quote about time as money is a perfect example of such philosophy:[6]

"Yesterday is a cashed check and cannot be used again.

Tomorrow is a promissory note and cannot be utilized today.

Today is cash in hand.

You have $86,400.00 (seconds) a day!

Spend/Invest them wisely!"

Time being a limited resource, Americans often experience great anxiety about making sure that time does not disappear on them. A person must strategize to not become a victim of such a kind of waste and its negative consequences.

Since success is so directly associated with the productive use of time, having time management skills is essential. In fact, time management skills have an almost mythical quality: You can blame anything that goes wrong—a work project, an exam, even a party—on an unfortunate failure of time management skills.

Because having time management skills is so important for overall success in life, the resources to learn such skills are everywhere. Books, articles, apps, webinars, corporate trainings, productivity coaches, techniques, shortcuts, you name it. An article on lifehack.com titled "18 Best Time Management Apps and Tools (2021 Updated)" provides an

---

6 http://michaeltay.com/338/seize-the-day-time-management/

example of the abundance of time management tools, and the associated pressure to use them: "If you're not taking advantage of some of the hundreds of time management apps and tools out there… you're definitely missing a trick."[7]

———

This means two things for your application. **First, you need to present yourself as someone who has made good use of time.** Your effective use of time in the past is a promise that you will also make good use of time in the future, when you have joined the organization you are trying to impress.

Second, you need to be cognizant that the people reading your application have limited time and attention to review your materials. In other words, your application must be clear and concise. For example, your resume must be direct and easy to read. You must arrive for your interview early (so that they don't waste time waiting for you) and never overstay your welcome.[8] Of course, you may be invited to stay longer at an interview than initially planned. But when in doubt, err on the side of caution. Offer to leave and explain it by saying, "I don't want to take more of your time."

Speaking of taking leave, if you are from a country less concerned with the productive use of time, you may have

———

7 https://www.lifehack.org/articles/technology/top-15-time-management-apps-and-tools.html
8 I watched this occur at a conference in the United States: A Brazilian academic was one of the panelists and she continued to talk well past her allotted time, apparently excited about how well she was doing. This caused great discomfort among the audience, as well as a terrible headache for the panel organizers, who had to find a way to fit the remaining panelists in the now much shorter time available to them.

the habit of saying goodbye several minutes before you actually leave. When I lived in Brazil, the unspoken rule was that you would mention it was time for you to leave, but then you would meander, perhaps talk about why you didn't want to leave but had to, perhaps even begin a new topic of conversation. Saying goodbye was a process.

In the United States, saying goodbye is brief. If you say you are going to leave, get up, say goodbye, and leave. Done.

Conversation beginnings have similar rules. When you meet someone in a professional setting, you are expected to make small talk, but it should be short and not delay the start of what you really came for. For example, if you just arrived for an interview, you are likely to be asked about the weather outside and whether you found the interview location easily. (If the environment is professional, you will not be asked about politics or religion. Sensitive subjects are simply out of bounds. Family matters should stay out of the conversation too.) This small talk is meant to "break the ice" and make everybody more comfortable before the serious tasks ahead. Small talk is simply a means to an end—the end being a productive meeting (see chapter "Productivity").

These "starting and ending" dynamics are valid not just for in-person conversations—whether one-on-one or in groups—but also for phone conversations, online meetings, and even emails. You want to say a brief hello and then get straight to business. If you come from a highly social culture, this can feel strange and even offensive. Over time, we learn that this is not personal, but just the result of living in a culture where time in professional settings is a commodity to be used carefully and productively.

PRACTICAL APPLICATIONS

1. All the documents delivered for an application must be easy to read and understand so that you don't waste the reader's time. This means that the language must be direct and clear, and the layout must be pleasant to the eye. An application that is confusing and requires that the evaluator reread to understand what you are saying will end up in the trash. (Not only that, but an unclear application can also indicate that you don't have the solid writing skills typically desired in an employment and educational context.)

2. Oftentimes, an application has parts with explicit instructions about a maximum number of characters (usually typed characters and spaces) or number of words you may submit. This limit is there because the evaluators don't have the time to read more than the determined amount of information. The best way to show that you understand and follow instructions (a desirable trait for any applicant) and that you respect the reader's time is to stick exactly to what is being asked.

3. Occasionally, an application will include an invitation to send additional, optional materials. In those cases, you can send that extra report, photo, or document that you feel would enrich your application. However, if such an invitation to send additional materials was not made, sending them anyway may serve as evidence that you don't pay attention to instructions and don't respect the evaluator's time.

4. Always use direct and clear language in your communications with those reviewing your application, even if the communication is just a simple email. For example, if you have a question that is not answered in the resources available online[9] and you need to send an email about it, write, "Hello, I'm writing to request…" rather than waste the reader's time providing more information than they need. Here is an example of such waste: "Hello, I was wondering if you could help me with a question that I have been thinking about for the last two days. I searched for the answer online in different ways, but everything I found was a little unclear. Could you please be so kind and send me more information about…"

5. Never use "lack of time" to explain anything that you may not have done. For example, do not say that you didn't get a good score on your TOEFL because you didn't have time to study. Lack of time is an insufficient excuse for anything, since you should have known how to better manage your time. If you didn't have time for this one task now, why should the person assessing your application believe that you will have time to do the tasks they would give you in the future?

6. Arrive on time for all meetings and early for interviews. If an interviewer has to wait for you at all, you essentially missed your chance to be considered, no matter your reason for not showing up on time. Problems such

---

9 It is important that you don't take anybody's time asking a question for which the answer is readily available. This would only demonstrate that you are a person who doesn't exercise their due diligence.

as transportation troubles are something you should have planned for.

7. Know how much time is available to you in a meeting or interview and respect the start and finish times. If it is not clear how much time you have available, try to find that information before you meet. This is not just so you can respect the other person's time, but also so you can better plan what amount of information you can fit into the time allotted.

8. One common way to indicate that you understand the value of another person's time is simply saying, "Thank you for your time." Even if the greatest contribution someone made was sharing their wisdom or advice, the "thank you" should still refer to their gift of time.

ALSO THINK ABOUT THIS...

- What is good time management for you? How do you accomplish it in your daily life?
- What strategies do you employ to manage your time and energy to avoid burnout?
- How do you expect to manage your time and your many responsibilities if you receive the opportunity you are hoping for?

5
PRODUCTIVITY

THE CONCEPT

In this chapter, we go deeper into the idea of doing more in less time, also known as "productivity." Why talk about productivity? Because in the United States, a good candidate is a productive candidate.

But first, what are we talking about exactly? The Cambridge Dictionary defines "productivity" as "the rate at which a person, company, or country does useful work."[10]

Rate is a measure of how many products are made or sold, or services delivered (and consequently money made), in the time it took to accomplish the task. Put simply, the goal of productivity is to gain more with fewer resources and less effort.

I'm going to digress a little to talk about productivity in business. But stay with me because this does matter for your application, and how will become clear later.

In business, productivity "is calculated by measuring the number of units produced relative to employee labor hours or by measuring a company's net sales relative to employee labor hours."[11]

---

10 https://dictionary.cambridge.org/dictionary/english/productivity
11 https://www.investopedia.com/terms/p/productivity.asp

For example, imagine a sandwich shop employee who makes 10 sandwiches in 10 minutes. This person is more productive than an employee at the same shop who makes 10 sandwiches in 13 minutes, right? The first employee is more productive because he or she took less time to deliver the same output—10 sandwiches.

Similarly, if a manager has a three-person team bringing in a million dollars in a three-month period, and another manager brings in the same million dollars in the same three-month period, but with a five-person team, the first manager is more productive.

Making more with less is productivity's main goal, whether the thing made is a $5 sandwich or a million-dollar project.

Now, these examples may give the impression that the only way to increase productivity is to make more with fewer resources. And I don't want you to have this narrow perspective because it will limit how you think about your own productivity as a candidate.

An alternative way to think about productivity is to do better things with fewer resources.

Remember that employee that makes a sandwich a minute? That quickly-made $5 sandwich may not be particularly tasty, but sometimes we don't mind basic if the price is right. Now let's picture a new employee in the same shop, but this person was hired to make "high-end" sandwiches. Let's say those "high-end" sandwiches take two minutes to make and are sold at $10 each. As you might have figured out, revenue for the establishment continues to be the same with the new employee, even if fewer sandwiches are being made and sold.

In other words, productivity can be attained in ways other than simply making more of something in less time.

The point is, there is more than one way to show productivity!

———

In the United States, and in other countries guided by similar economic and social principles, whether a person is or is not productive is laden with moral meanings.

Being productive is generally the sign of a "good person." It signals that the person is a go-getter, that they are hardworking, resourceful, and a creative problem solver. High productivity can earn the person respect and social standing in the eyes of others, including concrete rewards such as promotions, raises, and awards. In this context, being productive also produces feelings of accomplishment and self-respect.

Advertising campaigns encourage us to end the day, the week, or the year, with rewards such as a dessert, a purchase, or a vacation for all that we have accomplished. You can feel good and pat yourself on the back if you "went above and beyond."

Being unproductive, on the other hand, suggests a certain moral weakness. Whether the unproductive person did not have goals or had goals that could not be achieved, he or she risks being seen as lacking willingness and stamina to improve.

Judging the character of a person by their productivity is a widespread practice in the United States. However, this simplistic view disregards the fact that access to the tools that permit productivity—such as health, financial stability, access to transportation, information, and role models—is not the same for everybody.

You may have lacked access to such foundational supports in your life and this may have diminished your ability to be productive in the past. These deficits should only figure into your application if you can create a narrative of having overcome great odds to become more productive than most people under the same circumstances would be. The challenges you faced should not be used as an excuse for not having attained your maximum productivity level. That would only signal your inability to overcome obstacles, making you a less desirable candidate.

Because productivity is so important for a person to be successful, or at least be perceived as successful, the United States is fertile ground for productivity advice and hacks. They come in a variety of shapes, from productivity coaches (for individuals and whole companies) to organization-wide trainings, popular articles, blogs, books, and podcasts, to name just a few examples. This wealth of resources is awesome. But it also enforces the idea that low productivity is nothing but an inability to tap into solutions available to everyone.

People who are productive, especially despite great odds, are celebrated in stories, articles, and movies. Most of us don't even realize that this is the storyline we have been listening to our entire lives until we start paying attention. This infatuation with the highly productive hero points to America's preference for people who can demonstrate an ability to accomplish great things, no matter the conditions.

If conditions are detrimental to productivity, there are multiple ways to overcome them. Below are some strategies valued in the United States that can help you increase your productivity and also create a narrative about how you used to struggle with productivity until you found a way to address the problem. Such a story would demonstrate that you are able to reflect on what is holding you back, design a solution, and then implement it.

Let's take a look at some strategies Americans often use and recommend to increase productivity:

1. Avoid distractions. These can come in many shapes. If you are distracted by noises, such as a phone buzzing, you may need to turn off notifications. If the distraction is caused by children, you may need to arrange childcare. If your pet is distracting you, keep it out of your office. These external distractions are easy to notice and presumably easy to fix. If these solutions seem obvious, it is because they are. But in the United States, you want to present these as productivity tricks and not the obvious.

If the distractions come from inside your mind, in the form of worries and racing thoughts, you are dealing with a more elusive challenge. A stress-reduction program or a mindfulness and meditation practice could help. You may also find better control of your mind by engaging in a quintessentially American activity: the mind hack. Mind hacks are strategies that can trick your mind into doing something that it would not naturally want to do. For example, promise yourself that there will be a reward at the end of an unpleasant task and see yourself doing it more willingly than without the prize. The internet is filled with advice aimed at getting your mind to cooperate a little more. A search for "productivity mind hacks" should bring up an abundance of suggestions.

2. Understand the difference between being busy and being productive. In English, there is a term for being busy without really doing anything of value: "busy work." An example of busy work is when a substitute teacher gives students worksheets to fill out. This creates the impression that students are learning when what is really happening is more of a performance of teaching and learning.

Productivity guru and author of *The 4-Hour Workweek* Tim Ferris has said that the secret to success is trading being busy for being productive. How do you make that trade? One way is using technology, which has become a major source of shortcuts to increase productivity. For example, before adopting an automated scheduling system, I wasted a lot of time going back and forth with my clients to find a time to meet. This was especially difficult with clients in different time zones. Planning online trainings with people across several time zones was especially challenging. Then I began using an automated scheduling system! Now, each participant can sign in with their own time zone and automatically find out what time the training is offered in their time zone. Phew! This tool has allowed me to take back my time and certainly helped increase my productivity.

Other technologies used to improve productivity include project management tools and consumer relationship management (CRM) tools. For example, CRMs allow you to send a message (and maybe a special coupon) to a client on their birthday. This gives the illusion that the business made note of the client's birthday and remembered it because they care. It turns out that the message was automated and didn't cost the company a second or cent to create. It is well known that clients tend to buy from companies that they feel connected to. This little birthday reminder is a perfect productivity hack: more sales with no extra effort or time involved!

3. Maximize your productivity by using your time with purpose. My first exposure to this idea came when I was a young mom. My family and I were living in Brazil at the time, and my then only child had grandparents in the United States. When the baby was old enough to look at pictures, the grandparents sent a gift in the mail: a subscription to a monthly children's magazine called "Highlights." When the first issue arrived in the mail, I noticed something I had never seen in my country. Under the magazine name "Highlights" was a tagline that read "Fun with a Purpose"! (This magazine still exists today and, were it not for their ungenerous charge for my use of a cover image in this book, you would see it here. But I encourage you to look these cover images up online yourself.)

The tagline "Fun with a Purpose" indicated a promise in the magazine's very first contact with the child and caretaker: to offer not just a fun time, but also a purposeful time! Productivity, in the form of purposeful brain development, was embedded in the fun! I understood then that American children are encouraged to become ever better versions of themselves starting at a very young age. This is quintessential

America! (See chapter "Progress.")

Among adults in the United States, "fun with a purpose" also applies. A conversation with a stranger is not so much an opportunity to connect for fun as it is an opportunity to network. Networking is the work of connecting with others to serve your ultimate goal of becoming a more successful professional. Author Dan Sherman, in his book *Maximum Success with LinkedIn* puts it best: "I want as big a network as possible, since I don't know who knows someone who knows someone who can give me my next big opportunity." (See chapter "Elevator Pitch.")

As mentioned earlier, in this country, even taking a vacation can be framed as "fun with a purpose." When you rest and disconnect, you are also recharging your batteries, the same ones that were depleted by too much pressure at work. With recharged batteries, the vacationer can once again reach maximum productivity until the next depletion, which is then followed by a countdown to the next vacation.

4. To increase productivity, manage your energy output.
Imagine that you are trying to reach the top of a steep mountain. You could go fast and reach the top quickly but be totally exhausted by the end. Or you could learn techniques that make each step less tiring (and more productive in terms of ground covered) and breathing exercises that make each rest more efficient (more rest in less time). Productivity is about getting to greater heights, literally and figuratively, with less effort and in less time.

To better manage your energy expenditure in a professional setting you can use strategies such as taking a gym break mid-day, increasing your daily water intake, putting up inspirational quotes by your desk, and doing your hardest tasks when your energy is fresh in the morning. These are some of the energy management hacks that Americans often encourage in the workplace. These hacks can help increase productivity and counteract any undesirable tendencies to not get things done.

PRACTICAL APPLICATIONS

1. Examine your resume for places where you can add evidence of productivity. For example, perhaps you have "increased sales by 30%." To demonstrate true excellence in productivity, this increase should have happened in a period that your industry considers short. For example, you could add a timeline, like this: "The team increased sales by 30% in my first 6 months leading the department." Sounds much more impressive than the first version, right? Are there any "time" additions you could make to your resume that would reflect greater productivity?

2. Think about the productivity hacks that you may already utilize but may not even be aware of. For example, perhaps you have a morning routine that helps you feel strong and energized for the day. Are there ways you might incorporate such productivity hacks when you describe yourself in an interview? An interviewer may ask you directly, "How do you manage your time?" or something more subtle, such as "What is your work style?" or "What is your management style?" These are questions that invite

an answer about how you make productivity front and center in your life.

ALSO THINK ABOUT THIS...

- If you are dealing with productivity challenges now, this is the time to look at them and experiment with solutions. You want to have solved your productivity obstacles by the time you are a candidate for a competitive position.

6
EVIDENCE

THE CONCEPT

If you are applying for an opportunity in the United States, you need to know that this is the land of pragmatic people. And "evidence" is how such people know if something is true or false.

Let's look at an example. Say you were at a store and you had money to buy just one piece of clothing. But there were two nice pieces you were eyeing: a beautiful dress to use on special occasions and a pair of pants that were less exciting but would be very useful in your daily life. If you were a dreamer and romantic, you would be more likely to choose the dress. But if you were a pragmatic person, you would weigh the cost of each garment against its utility. You would consider things like the number of times you would wear each; the quality of the material; the comfort of the wear; and whether you already had the necessary accessories or would need to spend extra money on, say, matching shoes. If you were a pragmatist, you would look at all of that and decide to purchase what would give you the best return on investment (ROI): the pants.

A pragmatic culture naturally places more importance on knowledge gained from analyzing data than on knowledge based on intuition or feelings.

This explains, at least in part, why Americans like to see numbers before they will say something is true. Measuring something is the path to knowing it.[12]

Let me illustrate. When I was a young woman in Brazil, I checked my weight now and then on public scales available at pharmacies in my city. Since I didn't go to the pharmacy often, I usually had to "feel" if I had gained or lost weight. These days, we wouldn't say that we lost or gained weight without weighing ourselves first. In fact, we wouldn't dream of starting a weight loss regimen without owning a home scale where we could confirm that our dietary modifications were resulting in measurable change.

We could also record our daily weight in an app and chart it over time to see if there is a trend, and hopefully progress, toward a weight goal (see chapter "Success"). We could also record the calories we consumed each day and chart them in relation to our weight. The app could then analyze the data, with results delivering the truth about our body weight.

The possibilities for collecting data about ourselves are endless and have transformed the way we live in the United States. For example:

Perhaps you feel that you are walking a lot each day. But you won't be sure until you check your Fitbit.

---

12 I do realize that this does not apply to "controversial topics," such as climate change. The data is there, but too many Americans still have a hard time accepting its truth. I suppose pragmatism does not apply when the data is, to borrow from Al Gore, an inconvenient truth.

Maybe you feel rested when you wake up in the morning, but you won't know if you slept enough until you look at the clock and confirm that you have slept for your ideal number of hours. If you want to know if you are sleeping deeply enough, there are tools to measure that, too.

You may feel hydrated but won't know for sure if you consumed enough water in a day until you check the levels of liquid in your water bottle.

Perhaps you feel that you are becoming more popular on social media, but you won't know for sure until you check if your likes and followers have increased.

―――――――

Evidence is necessary not just to better know yourself, but also to better know the world around you. For example, you wouldn't invest in a company without being thoroughly familiar with its numbers. You wouldn't buy a car without checking its performance numbers against those of other cars.

Numbers is the name of the game. For example, colleges and universities often have a page called "[University name] at a Glance." You can find an example in infographic form from Syracuse University College of Law below.[13]

Notice how much you can learn about the institution in one quick look!

―――――――

13 http://law.syr.edu/uploads/docs/admissions/Infographic17-18_fnl.pdf.

Image used with permission from the Syracuse University College of Law.

Also note the line on top, "the value adds up," and the line on the bottom, "It all adds up to value." These phrases assure prospective students and families that the data presented points to "a good deal," that is, going to Syracuse Law will certainly pay off in the future. That is what a pragmatist would call a solid return on investment!

We said that evidence is knowledge based on data rather than feelings or intuition. Another way to think about evidence is knowledge based on facts rather than opinions.

These days, the difference between fact and opinion may appear to be muddled. All around us, people accuse each other of spreading "fake news"—news based on opinions rather than facts.

However, outside of politics, the difference between fact and opinion seems quite clear. In some schools, children learn about the difference between fact and opinion as early as third grade, as you can see in this image:

Image by Kelly Randal at teacherspayteachers.com

When I was teaching international college students about the United States, I often used ice cream to explain the difference. "I think salted caramel ice cream is the best!" is an opinion. I can't prove that it is the best, and plenty of people would disagree with me. There is room for debate, with arguments for and against. Opinions about taste can lead to lively discussions, as I'm sure you have experienced too.

Now let's say I'm interested in what is in the salted caramel ice cream from a local creamery. I don't want opinions about what might be in it. I want facts. An (invented) list of ingredients in the creamery's salted caramel ice cream might be: "23% milk, 38% cream, 5% caramel…" These facts could be proven through science-based analysis. There is nothing to debate here. The numbers are what they are, whether or not you like them or believe them. See the difference?

Just for fun, let's add another twist to this example. Look at this sentence: "In a survey conducted by the creamery in 2019, when presented with the choice between salted caramel or coffee ice cream, 69% of respondents reported preferring salted caramel ice cream, 25% reported preferring coffee ice cream, and 4% said they don't care for either." Is this a sentence about facts or opinions?

Although this is a sentence about people's tastes and preferences (opinions), the report itself is about facts. The phrase is a conclusion based on data and cannot be argued over. It can only be reproduced or challenged through a new survey.

Facts are firm. They are verifiable through an examination

of numbers, statistics, and even testimonials, as in court proceedings. A fact is never a little right. It is either right and can be proven, or it is not a fact.[14]

Why does this matter, you ask? Read on.

▨ **Knowing the difference between fact and opinion is essential if you want to successfully argue that you are the best candidate for an opportunity in the United States.**

Offering a circular explanation about why you are the best candidate will only bring you ridicule. You will simply not be taken seriously.

Can't picture an opinion in an application? Let's have some fun with an example and then improve it.

"I am the best candidate for this job because (1) **I know a lot about** (2) **supply chain management** and because (3) **I have worked in this field for many years**. In my current job, we have (4) **so many** (5) **top companies as customers**, you wouldn't believe it. Customers keep coming back for more (6) **because they love what we do.** (7) **I know what works**, and if I came to work for your company, (8) **I would know what works for your company, too.** I promise you it would grow a whole lot."

Ugh! Pretty bad, isn't it?

Now let's break it down and replace some generalizations in bold with fact-based, evidence-rich statements that are much more likely to help you make your case.

---

14 The difference between fact and opinion is a useful tool for the goals of this book. However, I do realize, together with other social scientists, that there are "human fingerprints" in even the most objective of facts.

1. **"I know a lot about…"** This means nothing unless you can present evidence. How much is a lot—did you take a weekend course or completed a Ph.D. with original research on the topic? Are you a recognized authority on the topic with X number of publications and/or Y years of experience? Be exact in your description if you want to convince someone you are an expert.

2. **"Supply chain management."** This is an overly broad field. To show rather than tell that you know the field, name your area of expertise within "supply chain management." One example would be "supply chain management, particularly trade management software in the food and beverage sector." This is much more interesting and credible than the general name of a field.

3. **"I have worked in this field for many years."** How many years? What were your job titles and/or responsibilities? Present facts and, if possible, demonstrate that over time your responsibility increased. Having supervisory responsibilities is typically seen as solid proof that you have more experience than others below you.

4. **"so many…"** How many? Two or three, approximately 50, 100, or a thousand?

5. **"top companies as customers"** Instead of claiming they are "top companies," cite their names, especially if they have good name recognition. I recently finished work for a client whose company serves Nike, Johnson & Johnson, and

Shell. Such "name dropping" (always based on facts) can promote your credibility without you having to say much.

6. "… because they love what we do." This can be said about anything. I go to the same bakery every few days because I love their bread. Not very impressive. Instead, describe what exactly keeps bringing your customers back. Maybe you even have customer satisfaction surveys, which could provide numbers about what your clients love.

7. "I know what works." This is a terrible statement. Instead, you want to be specific about solutions you have experience designing and implementing, and what specific problems you have solved. Provide examples, especially if they are similar to the challenges your interviewer is facing and wants an expert (like you) to solve.

8. "I would know what works for your company, too." This can give the impression that you think you know everything and are not open to learning about different circumstances. It is best to offer specifics on what you do have experience with and state that you expect that this experience will be beneficial for the resolution of their challenge.

Understanding the value of evidence and using it to boost your candidacy will already put you ahead of other applicants. Most people don't know how to present themselves in such a solid manner and resort to generic statements instead. You don't have to be one of them.

PRACTICAL APPLICATIONS

In addition to the practical examples given above, remember the following:

1. Leave any statements about feelings out of your application. For example, your letters of recommendation should focus only on your professional experience. Statements such as "I'm recommending Bob because he is a great friend" are irrelevant for the person assessing your professional qualifications.

2. In some countries, it is common to defend a position by simply making the same statement repeatedly, in different ways and at different times. In the United States, repetition is not appreciated, as it means wasted time and attention. Instead, replace repetition with data.

3. To present evidence, you will need to be up to date on your field. For example, you don't want to bring up expertise in a technology that is now obsolete. To show that you are capable of adding value to a company, you need to do research and show familiarity with what is current in the industry.

4. If you research your field, consider what agencies and organizations in the United States have the most respected data. To assess the reliability of a source, think about whether your interviewer would read that publication. If yes, you are likely safe using data from that source.

ALSO THINK ABOUT THIS...

- What are you most proud of in your career? Can these accomplishments be expressed in numbers? If yes, where can you find these numbers? How can you incorporate these numbers into your application?
- If you don't have numbers (some fields don't and there is nothing wrong with that), do you have other ways to prove facts? For example, have you presented papers at conferences that are recognized as significant? Are there people in positions of authority in your field who can vouch for you, so that their credibility becomes part of the evidence in your favor?

7

INDIVIDUALISM

THE CONCEPT

Remember learning in school about explorers who set out to sea from Europe to the Americas without knowing what they would find beyond? And then they, kind of by chance, "discovered" land? And they made it "theirs" through great difficulties?

Many of us memorized their names because—so we were taught—these heroes made the country. They courageously moved into the North American West, "sweeping aside the Native Americans."[15] Later, the "Founding Fathers" created the Constitution of the United States, and in the process the nation itself. This narrative is what many of us learned in school, not just in the U.S. but in international classrooms too.

I begin this chapter with a brief mention of the birth myth of the United States to show you that the idea of the hero who conquers all that is good in the world by himself is as old as the country itself. The foundation myth of the United States helps us understand who is admired in this country and therefore is valuable information for those who

15 True quote, from the textbook "American Ways: An Introduction to American Culture," which is still used in some American colleges and universities today.

want to create a positive impression on Americans.

You may be wondering why I call it a foundational "myth." Because left out of this narrative are the native communities who were the original inhabitants of this land and who played an essential role in the survival of the settlers— the same people who would cause their decimation. The native people of this land were not the beggars represented in the image of the colonial myth depicted above. Also left out of this narrative are the enslaved people abducted from Africa, whose forced labor led to the early wealth that made the United States the rich country it is today.

If we narrow our view even further, we can see that left out of this narrative are also the people who raised and encouraged the lone hero; the people who supported him financially, emotionally, spiritually, and even sexually; the people who educated him, made his tools, and patched his wounds. The members of the community making this one heroic existence possible are too numerous to count. And yet they are absent from the official account of how the country became the United States of America.

———

Many centuries later, most Americans continue to be culturally conditioned to credit a person's success only to their individual strength, courage, persistence, and grit. When obstacles happen, it is believed that those who have enough of those traits can overcome just about anything. Walt Disney famously said, "All of our dreams can become true, if we have the courage to pursue them." And who is more American than Walt Disney?

I'm critical of this position not because I don't think that individual characteristics such as courage and persistence matter. They certainly play a significant role in an individual's ability to fulfill their dreams. So do other personal traits such as the ability to problem-solve, to think outside the box, and to overcome obstacles. There is no doubt that these matter.

But the popular image of a winner who has—by his power alone—reached the top of the mountain is incomplete.

The list of factors that make us or break us is immense and goes well beyond whether or not we have the courage to realize our dreams.

This cultural emphasis on the lone hero that I am describing is not a simple curiosity about the United States. Instead, it has rather important implications for your application to opportunities in the United States.

The most obvious is that you must present yourself as a lone hero too. Your supporting cast should have a minor role or be left out entirely of the narrative about your accomplishments.

—————

As you have likely experienced, the work of turning dreams into reality can be tiring. This work can be especially exhausting when the culture keeps telling you that you should make it on your own. Denying the need for help, declining help when it is offered, and not joining forces to build a dream together puts a lot of weight on individuals.

When exhaustion sets in, Americans encourage each other to engage in "self-care." The term self-care refers to taking back time given to others and their priorities. It means spending time alone attending to what are understood to be more "authentic needs," such as more sleep, more attention to nutrition, perhaps time for relaxation with a pet or a good movie. Self-care is considered deserved self-indulgence, a time for giving oneself small pleasures and luxuries that would otherwise not be part of one's regular (and depleting) activities. These little luxuries and related products are often sold with promotional taglines such as "Self-Care is how you take your power back."

Congruent with a culture focused on the individual, the replenishing expected of this kind of care is done alone. Acts such as sharing our gifts with others or helping others attain their goals, as rewarding as they may be, are rarely considered a source of replenishment. Work done for others is by definition draining, hence the need to engage in the mending of one's own depletion through self-care.

Now, this is not to say that the United States does not value teamwork. Teamwork, and the general ability to be pleasant and productive in a group, is of utmost importance in the workplace, as well as in educational settings. This is the reason applications often contain a question about whether you work well with others.

Teamwork is valued inasmuch as it benefits the organization you are a part of; it does not reflect an inherent valuation of people being there for each other, helping each other grow. In fact, a manager that leads a team toward a successful outcome would then be better qualified to leave the team and get a higher position and higher salary somewhere else. Similarly, if a team wins a championship, the headlines are most likely to focus on the amazing performance of the team's star, who is now better positioned to get bought by a different and higher-bidding team.

In other words, even when teamwork takes place, the spotlight is still on the accomplishments of single individuals. And these individuals will be seen as successful not because they were helped by others but because they have the personality traits of a winner, such as courage and persistence. (See chapter "Success.")

If you want to be seen as a promising professional in the United States, you must present yourself as the one who braved the obstacles alone and came out, quite literally, on top. You must present your dream of working or perhaps studying in the United States as a professional and individual challenge and not as a family project.

I recently spoke with a client who applied for an EB2-NIW visa and received the dreaded Request for Evidence (RFE) from the U.S. Citizenship and Immigration Services (USCIS). The RFE asked why the candidate had written that he wanted to come to the United States to give his family a better future. Indirectly, they reminded the candidate that the United States is not in the business of giving families a better future. The National Interest Waiver visa is a visa to benefit the United States, not his family. And how was he going to do that, they wanted to know. If you are familiar with immigration processes, you know that an RFE can be expensive. Leaving your family out of the picture and justifying your interest in moving to the United States so that you may individually work for the interests of the country, that will please the officers much more!

PRACTICAL APPLICATIONS

1. Separate your professional from your personal life. If someone gave you a professional opportunity because they were a relative or a friend, mention the opportunity, but not the person who gave it to you. They prefer to hear that you gained the opportunity because of your superior abilities, not because of a friendship or familial obligation.

2. Refrain from mentioning family members in the initial stages of a candidacy. Information about your family is considered so private that American law prohibits your interviewer from asking questions about your marital status, family size, etc. The idea is that this is not only private information but also irrelevant to what matters: your qualifications for the job.

3. As mentioned in the chapter "Productivity," never use the needs of your family to justify not having had time to do well on a professional activity. Such a statement only signals that you don't know how to separate the personal from the professional.

4. When asked about your experiences and abilities to work in teams, remember that what your interviewer wants to know is not if you enjoy working with teams. Your likes

or dislikes are irrelevant. Instead, the focus should be on what you were able to accomplish because you were part of a team. If you led the team that accomplished a certain productivity goal, even better. Whatever the case, the focus should be on accomplishments and your role in them, rather than on the team members and your feelings about them.

ALSO THINK ABOUT THIS...

- At what points in your professional trajectory have you been supported by—perhaps even depended on—other people? After sending them your gratitude, consider how you can speak about your professional trajectory without mentioning these supporters.
- Did you ever stand out when working with a team? If so, how might you describe yourself as helping the team do something better/produce more of something than they would have been capable of accomplishing without you?

ALSO THINK ABOUT THIS...

8
PERSONAL BRANDING

THE CONCEPT

Recently, I was reading my local newspaper when I came across an interesting obituary headline: "Anything but Average: Lucille S. W., 1923-2020." I didn't know Lucille. It was not her remarkable life that called my attention. What caught my interest was that being "anything but average" is a goal that can accompany you all the way to your deathbed. Lucille's obituary reminded me of how much Americans dislike the idea of average.

There is a word, a flavor, that Americans use to describe that which is nothing special: vanilla. If you want to be seen for what you have to offer, if you want to stand out among the candidates for an opportunity, you must avoid being vanilla. You also want to avoid being a "wallflower," a person who blends in with the background.

A vanilla candidate is indistinguishable from the others. This person tells the interviewer they have encountered many obstacles in life but succeeded in spite of the odds—without giving any evidence. This candidate says that they are hardworking and always put their best into everything they do. Like everybody else who got this far? The interviewer probably expects nothing less from a viable candidate—this "trait" will not distinguish you from the pack.

———————

Personal branding is what you do to avoid seeming vanilla.

When working with clients, I often refer to the process of creating a personal brand as an exercise in increasing and lowering the volume of different parts of our lives. Think of your life as a very long musical piece. To self-brand effectively, we must carefully select what parts of the music to blast with fireworks, what parts to play in low volume, and what parts to mute entirely.

A successful application to anything in the United States requires that you be selective. Too often I see international applicants listing everything they have ever done in a resume, following the notion (common in some countries) that the longer the document, the more we have accomplished. In the United States, we must, instead, be extremely selective about what we show (the content) and how (the format) we show it.

Another good metaphor for this careful crafting of our image is the museum exhibit. Did you know that a museum has just about all the pieces of art it owns in a basement for safe-keeping? That collection is not curated and is not for public viewing. When an exhibit is prepared, that is when select pieces are brought up and arranged for viewing.

I invite you to think about your application as one specific exhibit. The pieces you bring up from the art museum basement for the exhibit are <u>the content</u>. The manner in which you arrange the pieces is <u>the format</u>.

In a museum, the person in charge of selecting the pieces and deciding how they will be arranged is the curator. Just like this professional, you will curate the exhibit of your career with care to select the best pieces and arrange them the best way possible, to create the impression that you want.

Curating your content and format is especially important in a country like the United States, where time is at a premium. (See chapter "Time.") Your application documents will probably receive just a few seconds of your reader's attention before they decide if they will continue reading or move on to another application. Your exhibit—the brand you present—must be strong and clear, or your materials will simply not get the attention they deserve.

———

If you come from a country other than the United States, you may have never heard the term "branding" applied to people. You may know "branding" as a term applied to products, and the art of branding as "marketing." For example, a recent online add by the Magnum Ice Cream brand reads "New Magnum Double Gold Caramel Billionaire Has Arrived."

Notice how the product is unabashedly not vanilla! It is gold! It is not millionaire, but billionaire, with a <u>b</u>! It is not single, but double! More, more, more, says the American consumer, as he reaches for a box of Magnum ice cream bars instead of its average competitor.

Is this ad over the top? Yes. Is it unusual? No. So if you

think that you can't show off your gems without being "too much" in the United States, think again!

In this culture, people who want to be successful are expected to create a brand for themselves. Dan Sherman makes it explicit in his book about LinkedIn success: "Everyone has a brand. I am talking about You, Inc. What do you want to be known for? What's your specialty? What sets you apart?"

Yes, this may sound unrefined, even crass. But, whether you like self-branding or not, you do need to communicate your unique qualities so you can stand out among your competitors. Why should a company or university choose you rather than others? It is your job to help the gatekeepers find the answers to this question with the least effort possible.

If you are still unsure about branding yourself, you should know that awesomeness is encouraged from a very young age!

Image used with permission from Mint and Orange on Etsy.

If even after reading this, you are still on the fence and would rather present your qualities quietly and hope to get noticed, remember this: The opportunity you want but will not get will not just disappear into thin air. This opportunity will just simply be given to someone else! So, whenever the fear of self-branding stops you, imagine this other person getting the opportunity you wanted because they weren't afraid to show what distinguishes them from the competition. Then go be that person rather than the competition left behind!

Having established that standing out among other candidates is critical, let's dive deeper into some ways you can set yourself apart.

Your first job is to select what you will show in your museum exhibit. What is **the best content** you have available to display?

Whether you are preparing a resume, a cover letter, or practicing for an interview, the guidance is the same: Don't bring your entire life up but look at the events of your life and select the elements that best show that you were made for the opportunity in front of you.

Let's look at three strategies to select the best content.

1. Decide what employment you will show (and not show) in your exhibit. I have clients who have already moved to the U.S. and are now working in jobs that are unrelated to the career they had in their home country and that they aspire to practice in the United States. If you are a highly qualified individual in your country and you are looking to do similar work in this country, it is best to leave unrelated positions out of your resume. They don't add to the personal brand you are creating and they can distract from your awesome accomplishments in the past.

Perhaps you worry that, if you don't show all these other jobs you have had, there will be a gap in your resume. There are numerous ways to fill such gaps and thus show that you have continued to grow in your field. For example, you can take courses, attend conferences, volunteer in your field, and engage in shadowing assignments. Even if those are just a small portion of your week, these activities show that you have continued to seek growth in your field. Americans tend to be very understanding and lenient if they see that a person is genuinely striving to progress even in the smallest of ways.

2. Be selective in other parts of your exhibit as well.

Perhaps during your undergraduate training you engaged in internships or practicums. Perhaps you also held summer jobs, externships, or had shadowing opportunities in your field. If you are eyeing a spot at an institution of higher education or at a company that values practical experience, you want to bring all these experiences to your exhibit, even if they didn't last long. This is because the collection of these efforts shows consistent interest and investment in building up your practical experience.

If, however, you are eyeing a position that requires less practical experience, you might choose to leave some of the minor experiences out of your exhibit. This will free up space to show more about another area that might be more valued by a particular reviewer.

3. Silence what is not impressive.

When you are lacking in a certain area of your exhibit, it is better to not mention it at all than to show something lackluster. For example, if you have a lot of volunteer experience in your professional field, it is worth creating a "Volunteering" header to showcase these experiences. But if you have only volunteered for a few hours a couple of times in your life, it is best to leave such a header out. Silence not only removes what is less desirable from the picture, it also allows the reader's attention to remain focused on the more impressive material.

These are just a few strategies that will help your reader get excited about your brand. And if you are still hesitant about leaving some information out of your exhibit, remember that by being selective you also protect your reader's time. And Americans will always appreciate that—and perhaps even reward it.

———

Once you have selected the pieces that best create the brand you want to be known for, you then need to choose the best way to frame these pieces. (This is the format we referred to earlier.)

Let me share a short story about frames. I once was in a coffee shop in a small but tourist-drawing town and noticed a young local artist arranging her art on the walls for an exhibit opening later that day. In walked a well-known artist from New York City, and when he saw the young woman putting her frames up, he walked over to her. He proceeded to give her a lesson about framing that applies to our discussion about to best present information.

From my seat, I heard this well-established artist telling the local artist that he was fortunate to be able to make a living from his art. Then he asked if this was her desire, too. She replied, "Yes, of course." He replied: "Then you have to pay attention to your frames!" He told her that her frames looked cheap and that this made her art look cheap. "When a frame is second-class, the viewer naturally expects the art the frame holds to be inferior," he said. "The frame sets the tone," he explained. "This is not good or bad, just human nature." He said that the same art that looks cheap in a shabby frame can look fabulous and expensive when placed in a high-quality frame. With one, you don't make a living. With the other you do. It's that simple!

Of course, there are other factors that impact whether something sells or not. But it is also true that how we frame something—how we format it—has a larger impact on how the thing inside is perceived than most of us realize.

When you prepare the exhibit of your accomplishments, you must select the best pieces available. But it is equally important that you arrange these pieces in a way that enhances their value.

Here are some formatting strategies that can help.

1. Present what your audience values the most first. The top left, where the eye hits first (at least in Western cultures), is "prime real estate." This is the place for the most valuable information in any written document. The bottom right, where the eye hits last, is where we should put information of less value, like the page number in a resume.

But what deserves the top spot?

The deciding factor should always be who your audience is and what your audience values the most (see chapter "Audience"). Too often I see clients thinking about what they like best about their resumes and emphasizing that. Instead, we should consider what the people reading our applications value more and emphasize that.

For example, consider your audience when you decide whether to list the institution you attended first or the degree you earned first. Institutions with solid name recognition should be listed before the name of your degree. However, if the institution is less well-known, but your degree is a Ph.D., it is probably best to list the degree first.

2. Know what your audience values less and, if "less" is all you got, find a way to transform it into gold. A while back, I worked with a dentist who had done most of his professional work in the area of facial harmonization, a specialization that emphasizes improving a person's looks. This dentist was applying to a position in the United States, a country where working to make someone's face more beautiful is valued less than, for example, helping a child correct a dental malformation that has caused them to be bullied their whole lives.

Instead of showing him as working in aesthetic dentistry,

we presented him as focused on restorative dentistry, as well as oral and maxillofacial surgery. Same activity but presented in a way that made him more valued by the audience that mattered.

In his personal statement, we did have to address the years of experience he had in facial harmonization. We then explained that this was a financial choice that came out of the need to pay for his student loans and dental office equipment. Now that these expenses were covered, he was looking to pivot to this other (more noble) area, which had been his life's desire all along. Same information, just presented in a much more attractive manner for this audience.

As you have probably noticed by now, personal branding is not for the faint of heart. Many people are uncomfortable promoting themselves. Whether this comes naturally to us or not is likely a product of our personality and of the culture in which we were raised. I have an international friend here in the U.S. for whom just making eye contact takes an enormous effort. Where she came from, this is impolite. Shaking someone's hand with confidence is even more difficult for her. Then to self-brand? Forget it!

So, you may need to push yourself out of your comfort zone to get to that sweet spot, where personal branding feels authentic and not a form of bragging.

Self-branding is not bragging. Bragging often includes being loud unnecessarily, going on an ego trip, and announcing that you are awesome and perfect. Braggers exaggerate and come across as insecure.

Personal branding, on the other hand, requires being humble and presenting the best that you can offer in a light that is flattering and solid. That solidity comes from evidence—data that speaks for you.

PRACTICAL APPLICATIONS

1. It (almost) goes without saying that, no matter how great your self-branding is, if your materials contain grammar mistakes, you will be perceived as someone who is not ready to succeed. Grammar mistakes are especially inexcusable in this era when online grammar checks are easily available. Even minor mistakes can have a substantial impact, not necessarily due to the size of the mistake itself, but because they signal something bigger: that you are a careless person.

2. Personal branding can take place when you introduce yourself to a potential employer, investor, or admissions director, as well as on many other occasions. To get ready for any such situation, you need to create an elevator pitch (see chapter "Elevator Pitch").

3. Throughout your career, but especially when you are starting out, consider who among your connections might be willing to speak or write on your behalf in the future, and then stay in touch with these people. If you go to the same conferences, for example, share a coffee or drink and catch up. These warm connections can become priceless in the future.

ALSO THINK ABOUT THIS...

- How do you feel about self-branding? If showing your best to others makes you anxious, you may need help from a professional. This can come in the form of a therapist (if you have time on your side and the block is mostly emotional) or a professional writer (if you are short on time and/or it is a matter of skills you never developed). Often, an outside observer is better able to sing your praises than you would do for yourself.

- If you don't think you have much to show, enlist relatives and friends and ask if they remember anything you might have told them about an accomplishment and/or recognition in the past. It is common for those close to us to remember things we have forgotten, and they can help jog our memory.

PART 2:
APPLICATION MATERIALS

9
YOUR AUDIENCE

Your audience is the people who will read and consider your application. Like the audience in a theater, they are the people who will leave the performance enchanted, annoyed, or silent. The sentiment that you evoke with your performance is the difference between you getting the opportunity you want and being forgotten.

Here are three tips that will help you shape your performance and earn acclaim:

First, know your audience to the core. Know not just their values and the cultural expectations of their country, but also the culture of their organization.

It used to be that you couldn't find out much about the culture of an organization until you were actually part of it. Today you can access such information much sooner and with less risk. The internet has plenty of resources to find out more about what an organization values. Say you are trying to understand a program at a university that you hope to join. You should begin by studying the website of the university and of the program itself. Look for how they describe themselves, what they emphasize, and what they don't mention. (Yes, what is absent is also telling!) Dig deeper to find out the courses they teach and who the professors are. Look for what the professors research and what they publish. You may even have a chance to see them speak in a professional conference. These are all valuable resources to understand what motivates an organization and the people in it.

If your purpose is to understand a business, study their website as well as sites that provide data about well-known businesses. You can also study the profiles of the business leaders on sites such as LinkedIn. See what they talk and write about and what they comment on. Look for people and organizations they associate with. You can examine how the business is reviewed by consumers and by employees, anonymously, on sites like www.glassdoor.com. Such resources are invaluable.

Second, present what you have to offer in a manner that responds to what the audience is looking for. For example, if a university program states that they prefer students just out of college, and you graduated 20 years ago, don't waste their time or yours. Find a program that is a better fit and put your time and attention into that application instead.

Let's look at some different audiences and how this tip works for each.

If your audience is an employer, show how your training and experience have prepared you to help them solve a problem they have (as described in the call for applicants).

Remember, they are not searching for a new hire for fun. They are searching because they have a challenge and they would like to solve it with the least amount of resources.

If your audience is a college or university, use your application to tell them what you want to learn from them and why you are choosing them over other programs. (Remember, it is human to like flattery.) Show how much you have accomplished, but also be clear about how much more you need and are looking forward to learning. Convey that you are an independent student (as well as a great team player, of course), that is, you will not cause them undue trouble and stress.

If your audience is an immigration authority, be clear about what you have to offer the country and show evidence of that. Your application is not being considered because you are nice or because you always dreamed of living in the United States. Such statements will actually damage your application. The United States only opens its doors if it is to the country's advantage. Show them that giving you the visa you seek is to their benefit.

Third, no matter the audience, be sensitive to the fact that many Americans are attached to the notion that the United States is number one in the world, and that immigrants come to this country simply because they are attracted to such greatness. Therefore, even if you are an expert, say, in an innovative technology that can aid Americans, it is best not to present yourself as someone who can bring something better to the U.S.

Instead, it is best to present yourself as someone who can contribute to something that the country is already doing. For example, you can say that you have experiences that have prepared you to effectively collaborate with their team to find better solutions. You can state that you are looking forward to adding knowledge you acquired at X, Y, or Z to their already impressive resources. You can say that you aim/are well-prepared to help expand the offerings that the company is developing. You can state that you trust that your experiences in [your country] would enrich the learning experience of others at X university. In all of these cases, you are presenting yourself as capable and willing to help something already strong get stronger. And that is much easier for Americans to welcome than someone they might perceive as a "show-off."

10
YOUR RESUME

You can easily find guides on how to write an American resume online and in books. My goal in this chapter is not to reproduce what has already been done, but to call your attention to issues I often encounter when working with international professionals. Some of the points raised have received a more thorough treatment in other parts of the book. But I mention them again here so that each chapter can stand alone. If you need to quickly create a resume, this chapter can serve as your main reference.

First things first. You are probably working on a resume, not a curriculum or a CV. Most people think these are the same thing, and this may be the case in your country. In the United States, there are important differences.

A curriculum refers to the content of an educational program. It means a collection of lessons, as in "the biology curriculum at the Greylock high school is excellent."

A CV, short for Curriculum Vitae, is a document similar to the resume in that it lists educational and professional activities. The difference is that the CV is for academics, that is, people who engage in scholarly activities such as research and publishing, teaching in colleges and universities, holding leadership positions in these institutions, giving talks, and organizing professional panels. To list these, the academic needs a lot more space than the one to two pages of a resume. The formatting will also have different requirements than the resume. In other words, unless you are an academic, you don't need a CV.

A resume is the document that most of us need when we are applying for opportunities in the United States. Below, I provide an overview of formatting and content for a chronological resume. (There are variations, such as the functional resume, in which work experience is grouped by type rather than by year. But the chronological resume is most common and that's the reason we focus on it here.)

A common misconception about resumes is that they are documents that list everything a person has ever done in their life. According to this logic, a short resume is for people who don't have much experience and a long resume is for the truly successful professional. This view is mistaken, at least in the United States.

Now, it is important to note that everybody should have a document in which they list everything they have ever done, every course ever taken, and every prize ever received. (It's just that this document is not your resume.) Each entry in this collection of everything you have ever done should include details such as the name of a course or position, what institution offered it, and where and when it took place. If there were quantifiable results associated with the entry, such as an increase in something desirable or reduction in something undesirable, list those too. I call this document a Base Resume.

Following the museum exhibit metaphor presented in Chapter 8, think of the Base Resume as the basement of an art museum where all art pieces owned by the museum are kept and cataloged. A resume for a specific opportunity is like one exhibit in that museum, not the entire museum. Every exhibit shows a curated selection of all that the museum owns—this selection is chosen with purpose, according to very specific criteria. For example, an exhibit about Picasso should not include the dinosaur replica the museum owns. For an exhibit about Aretha Franklin, the Picasso should stay in the basement.

ABOUT FORMATTING

There are many ways to format a resume, from the more traditional horizontal layout to two or three columns, and you can be more or less adventurous depending on your audience. For example, if you are applying for an opportunity at a university or company that is well-established and proud of its history, chances are you will do better with a traditional resume. If you are applying for an opportunity in the creative sector, a more experimental resume can give your reader a taste of your original personality. If you want examples, just do a search online and many formatting options will pop up. See what speaks to you, consider the values of the institution you want to join, and make your choice.

Regarding format, there is one other issue that is often neglected: Though you do want to present a lot of information in a small space, you also want to make sure your document is easy on the eye. How do you do that?

First, format should be consistent throughout your resume. Whether spacing, font type and font size, or date formatting, everything should be easy to understand with just a quick look.

Second, you need some white space between items and

around the margins so that the eye can move through the document without the unpleasant feeling of constriction caused by crammed resumes. This means that, if you must choose between a crowded one-page document with practically no margins or a lighter two-pager, go with the latter.

Third, remember to list your entries from the most recent to the oldest. This is the expectation, and your reader will need to work harder to understand what you have accomplished if you change the rules of the game.

ABOUT CONTENT

Now that you know how to format, let's look at what should be included in your resume. This part of the chapter is organized by different headers: some you must include—marked with an asterisk—and others are optional.

The Top*

In some countries, the top of a resume includes personal information such as date of birth, marital status, and ID numbers.

This is simply not done in the United States. If you do just one thing recommended in this chapter, go remove any personal data other than your name and contact information from your document as soon as possible.

Why? Because—technically at least—you should be assessed for a position purely on your skills and merits. Your age (date of birth), your marital status, and whether or not you have children should be irrelevant to the person evaluating your qualifications. In the United States, you have the right, by law, to be assessed on your merits alone. (Of course that is the ideal and not always reality.)

On the top of the page you should include only your name, possibly degree initials after a comma, and then information about how you can be contacted: one email, one phone number, and an address, if where you are located is important to the position.[16] Increasingly, we are seeing resumes that do not include an address, indicating that the person is free to relocate or is a digital nomad and location does not impact their ability to fulfill the responsibilities of the position.

The Summary or Profile
Whether called a Summary or Profile (or Professional Summary or Professional Profile), this is the first header after your name and contact information. This section presents the highlights of your resume, with the goal of keeping the reader interested in the details available in the sections that follow. This is truly a summary, so keep it short. You can choose to write it in a narrative format or in bullet points, whatever seems more attractive and easier on the eye.

I personally like to write this section last, when the work on the rest of the resume is complete and the gems of the resume have become absolutely clear.

Work Experience*
This section can also be called Professional Experience, Work History, Professional History, or another variation. For each entry, list your title, name of the organization or business that employed you, city and state (and country, if not the

---

16 Why not all your emails and phone numbers? Because in case the reader needs to contact you, they have no way to assess which of the choices is best. This causes distraction and inefficiency.

U.S.), and from when to when you were there. It is best to list month and year of start to month and year of end, unless you were at the same employer for so many years that months don't make a difference. If you are self-employed, simply list the name of your business and use a job title that makes it obvious that you are the owner and head of the organization.

Depending on your field of work, you may want to include a brief description of what the organization or business does, and also list your responsibilities in more detail.

Education*

Here you want to list any undergraduate (college or university) and graduate (university) studies you have completed that have led to a degree. Do not list your high school education, as this would be part of your basic education and not education toward a career—the focus of a resume.

For each entry in this section, list the name of the degree you obtained, the educational institution that granted it, graduation year as in "Class of 2007", or year of start and year of conclusion. If your degree included internships and externships, also list them here as part of your Education, not under Work Experience. The only exception to this rule is if you have no professional experience outside of educational settings. In this case, you are permitted to list internships, externships, shadowing, and so on under Work Experience.

Do not list the number of hours for undergraduate degrees (Bachelor's) and graduate degrees (Master's and Ph.D.). At least in theory, they should involve a similar workload across countries.

When it comes to post-graduate degrees, however, the variation in the number of hours can be great—I have seen anywhere from 120 hours to 2,100 hours. This is why listing credit hours for these entries is important. Check your diploma to find the exact number of credit hours to add to your resume.

Note that in both Work Experience and Education, you have the option of listing the name of the position/degree **or** the name of the institution first, depending on what you want the reader to pay more attention to. This, again, is a decision that should be based on your audience and what they value the most.

Professional Development

Here you list relevant educational activities that enhanced your skills but did not lead to a degree. Each entry begins with the name of the professional development activity (such as the name of a course), the institution that offered the activity, where it took place, and workload (number of hours).

Remember to also list the month and year it started and the month and year it ended (like Aug 2020-May 2022). If it was an activity that took place within the same year, but different months, list month to month and year (Aug-Dec 2021). If it was an activity that took place within a few days, list month, day-day, and year (Aug 8-10, 2021). If the activity took place on one day only, list the month, day, and year (Aug 9, 2021). A reminder: Americans always expect the month to come before the day of the month.

Just as above, it is a good idea to also list the city, state, and country (if not the U.S.) where the activity took place. This lends the development activity credibility, since technically with this information the reader could verify that the institution exists and offers the activity you are claiming it does.

In some professions, these continuing education activities are quite common, and you may have dozens to list. Since your space is limited, consider listing only those with more than a certain number of hours (I suggest four hours as the cutoff). You can always add the word "Select" or "Highlight" before or after "Professional Development," indicating to the reader that this is only a partial list.

Licenses and Certifications
You may list licenses and certifications that add to your professional credentials here. But remember that some certifications may be valuable in your country but have an obscure meaning for your American reader. In this case, it is best to leave this header out, and use the space for information that serves you better.

Professional Memberships or Associations
These professional affiliations are highly valued in the United States. Such associations are different from licensing bodies: You join them out of a desire to remain abreast of developments in your field and not because you need them to be able to practice your profession. These voluntary memberships typically require the payment of annual dues and come with benefits, such as subscriptions to specialized publications and conference discounts. Membership in such associations is an excellent way to show professional commitment and credibility to your American readers.

Publications

Publications demonstrate that you are a professional worth listening to. Articles in professional journals and book chapters or entire books dedicated to a topic in your profession are best, but write-ups about your work or text authored by you in popular publications are also valuable.

Media Appearances

If you have any media appearances where you discussed your work, such as interviews, list those, including the topic, the avenue, the date of the event, and, if possible, a link to a recording or other documentation about the event.

Public Speaking

If part of your professional credibility comes from speaking engagements, list them here, including the topic of the talk, location, and date(s). If you have too many to list, remember the words "Select" or "Highlights" can be added, to show that there is more.

If your speaking engagements took place at professional conferences, remember that events of international and national reach are more impressive than local events. If you don't have space to list everything, always choose the events with widest reach.

Recognitions or Awards

Only list these if they are related to the professional credentials you are promoting in the document. Besides listing the usual—name of the award, organization granting it, and where and when—include a brief explanation of what the honor represents (for example, it is a local, regional, or national award) and what you accomplished to be selected for this honor.

Volunteer Activities
Here you list work you have done without pay that has benefited others. This is hopefully in your field, but other volunteering may be of value to your reader as well. List your role in the volunteer opportunity, the organization sponsoring the activity, city, state, and country (if not the U.S.), from when to when, and who benefited.

Languages
You can add this heading if you know more than your native language. Ideally you should include English here, but if your English is not advanced, it is best to leave this heading out to not call attention to your (current but short-term) limitation, especially if you are applying for a position where you would be interviewed in English. Begin the section listing your "native language," followed by these exact words (as in French – Native Language). For each additional language, list the name of the language and your general level, as in "Advanced," "Intermediate" or "Beginner." I don't use the word "Basic" to describe language knowledge because it implies that you are stuck at that level. "Beginner," on the other hand, suggests a work in progress that may soon become "Intermediate" and then "Advanced."

These are the basics of an American resume!

11

COVER LETTERS, PERSONAL STATEMENTS, AND MORE

No matter what you are applying for, you will typically be required to produce an additional document that spells out why you are interested in a specific opportunity. This document has different names depending on the opportunity, and their content will vary as well.

If you are applying for a job, you will need a cover letter.[17] This document should include these five items:

- Where you learned about the position.
- What draws you to the position.
- How you would contribute to the employer.
- What past education and work experience qualify you to make such contributions.
- How you can be reached.

---

17 Sometimes simple jobs will only ask for a resume. But for most of the readers of this book, this will not be the case.

Do not to present a summary of your resume in the cover letter. Instead, study the position you are applying for in detail and address the requirements of the position in your cover letter directly. It is also a good idea to study the potential employer's culture and make references to their priorities in your cover letter.

Remember, they are looking to hire someone because they have a need. The cover letter is the opportunity for you to explain, always with evidence, why you are an excellent person to fill that need.

A couple of wording matters in the cover letter:

- Do not introduce yourself as someone looking for work. That diminishes your power. Instead, describe yourself as someone who is looking to contribute to the company. This puts you in the driver's seat: "I can contribute, and I hope you will let me do so." (Subtext: And if you don't, I will just go contribute somewhere else.) Can you see the difference?
- Do not describe what the job would mean to your life or why it would be perfect for you. The prospective employer is not looking to please you. Instead, describe what you can do for the employer, which is why the opening was created in the first place.
- Do not introduce yourself as the best candidate they will ever find. That can sound conceited. Instead, describe yourself as someone with a unique combination of skills and experience that is highly valued in the industry but unusual among candidates. With such a statement, you are putting yourself above the

competitors not because you say so, but because the evidence and the market say so.

If you are applying for a program at an educational institution, you will need a Personal Statement (or Statement of Intent), Intent Letter, College Essay, or variations on the theme.

This document is much less prescriptive than a resume or cover letter. Here you are expected to show more of yourself and your qualities as a person. The institution has likely already received your grades and/or transcripts and test scores, such as the TOEFL. Through these documents, they know who you are as a scholar. Now they want to know who you are as a person (and as a writer).

For this reason, this document should include at least a bit about a significant and, perhaps, transformative time in your life that led you to know yourself and/or the world in a new way. This account should be rich in detail so that the reader can picture it in their mind and accompany you on your journey.

Ultimately, this account of an important event or moment in your life should demonstrate your ability to learn, grow, and transform into a better person. The "better" can come in many forms (see chapter "Progress"): more confident, more persistent, more aware of a problem and committed to its solution, more determined to follow a certain career path… The possibilities are endless.

The story should help your reader understand the source of your interest in a certain field of study. Or, if the relationship between these two is not direct, your story should at least illustrate the kind of learner you would be in the classroom and the kind of community member you would be at the educational institution.

I find that this document requires just as much artistry as writing a poem or creating a painting. You can approach it from so many angles, and even after you have determined what story you want to use, deciding how to use it is another creative act.

There is another layer of complexity to this document: You are being assessed not just for what you have written but also for how you write. Your statement is an unofficial writing sample that shows your abilities as a writer. Since academic activity, in general, requires a great deal of writing, your reader wants to see high-quality writing. Do a poor job putting your sentences together, and your score on your application will get knocked down, no matter how interesting your story!

Think of this document as a painting. It must entice the viewer with excellent colors and composition—your story and how you present it. But the theme of the painting must also be powerful and relevant for the viewer—the narrative about the contributions you would make to the institution. Lastly, the painting must demonstrate that you are technically savvy in the use of the colors and the brush—the quality of your writing. It's a tall order, but it can be done if you give this document the time and attention it requires.

If you are applying for an immigration visa called the EB2-NIW (National Interest Waiver), you will be required to write a Professional Plan, which your attorney may also call a **Proposed Endeavor**. (If you are applying for this visa and plan to open your own business in the United States, you will need to submit a business plan instead. Consult with your attorney.[18])

The EB2-NIW is a visa that allows the recipient to live and work in the United States without the need for a prior arrangement with a U.S. employer who serves as a sponsor. It is quite literally a visa given to those who have skills and experiences that are of national interest to the country. The reasons for that national interest vary. For example, you may be a worker in a field that is expected to grow in the United States beyond the country's capacity to fill such need with domestic workers. Or the country may already be experiencing a shortage of the type of skills you have and is unable to train new people fast enough to avoid a crisis in the sector. All these would be reasons for the United States Citizenship and Immigration Services (USCIS) to consider granting an EB2-NIW.

Since this visa focuses on National Interest, a Professional Plan must link your skills and experience to the national need you propose to help fill. A Professional Plan must not just demonstrate that you have skills and experience, but also indicate beyond a shadow of a doubt that your skills and experience are urgently needed in the U.S. In other words, your documents must show that you are the solution to a problem faced by the country today.

---

18 Please, be reminded that I am not a lawyer and this description of the EB2-NIW visa does not constitute legal advice. I simply write documents for clients and for lawyers submitting these kinds of visa applications, and this is how I learned about what is preferred for the granting of the EB2-NIW visa. However, USCIS officials are famous for not following clear evidence, sometimes even denying the EB2-NIW for a highly qualified candidate in an area of need and granting the EB2-NIW for a person in the same field who is less experienced. Luck is, unfortunately, still a factor in whether the evidence presented in documents such as the Professional Plan will be considered carefully.

12

RECOMMENDATION LETTERS

The very first thing you should know about recommendation letters is that, technically, you are not supposed to see them. Yes, most recommenders will share what they wrote with you. That's because usually they care about you, and they know it will make you happy to read all the great things they wrote about you. (Or they may even tell you they want you to write the recommendation letter for them, and they will just review and sign. This is a lot more common than institutions will admit.)

However, officially, you must decline to see the letter. This fact is so important that there may be a question on your application forms that asks if you waive the right to see the recommendation letter. You should <u>always</u> check the box that confirms that "yes, I waive my right to see the letter."

This is a formality, but an important one. The idea is that because you didn't see the letter, the recommender could write truthfully, including any concerns they might have about you as a candidate. Of course, typically we wouldn't ask for recommendation letters from people who think badly about us in even a minor way. When a person accepts the request to write a letter of recommendation for you, there is a tacit agreement that they approve and support your candidacy. (If someone declines to write a letter of recommendation because of "lack of time," even if this is just an excuse because they have a less than 100% favorable view of you, respect their reason and move to the next potential recommender.)

Now that you know how to handle recommendations, let's talk about what criteria to consider when choosing potential recommenders. If you have a choice of people to ask for a letter, it is typically best to approach people who know you well and:

- are experienced professionals in the same field as you. This person should know how the field works and be able to write authoritatively about how your work has contributed to it in the past and present, and how they expect you to contribute to it in the future.
- have respected credentials that prove they are an authority in the field. What great credentials mean typically depends on your field, but generally we consider factors like level of education and reputation of their university, jobs they have held, leadership positions they have occupied, and any other demonstration that they are experts of some kind.
- have known you professionally for a long time (not "since I was a child" kind of long time), so that they may speak about your growth over time. For obvious reasons, a letter from someone who has known you professionally for several years will generally be more valuable than a letter from someone who has known you for just a few months.

- are reliable enough to write the letter they said they would. Applications have deadlines and an enthusiastic recommender who doesn't write a letter or doesn't post it in time is of no use to you.

When you have selected whom to ask for a letter of recommendation and received their approval, you may find yourself in one of two situations:

1. The recommender says they will be happy to write the letter. Thank them sincerely, then give them a copy of your most current resume. If this is an application for a job, it is good to share the job description and your cover letter. If it is an application for a university, it is good to provide your statement of purpose or a similar document to help guide your recommender.

2. The recommender says they will be happy to review and sign whatever you write. This kind of carte blanche is particularly common with recommenders who know you well, have little time, don't know what the requirements are for a letter of recommendation for an institution in another country, or don't write comfortably in the language your letter needs to be written in. This situation is common for people for whom this book is written.

If you are in situation number two, what is next? Here are some options:

First, you can write a recommendation letter in your original language, have your recommender review and approve it, and then pay someone to translate from your language to English. The problem with this solution is what we discussed in the first chapter of this book: When words alone are translated, the cultural expectations fail to be addressed. In other words, cultural obstacles can seriously prevent a translated letter from shining.

Here is a real-world example: Your recommender holds the title of Adjunct Professor in your country. In some countries, being an Adjunct Professor is a very respectable position, akin to an Assistant or Associate Professor in the United States. However, in this country, an Adjunct Professor is at the bottom of the academic ladder. Adjuncts get paid very little; they are hired and paid by the class, with zero job stability and benefits. In fact, an adjunct's pay (by course) can be so low that some adjunct professors in the U.S. need to resort to government food assistance programs to simply be able to feed themselves! (I bet you didn't know this was possible in American academia, right?) Now, imagine your professor's title was translated as Adjunct Professor in a recommendation letter for a top university in the United States. That letter just lost a great deal of value, don't you agree? A culturally aware translation would have titled the professor correctly and been a much stronger endorsement of your application than the endorsement from what appears to be a low-tier professor.

Second, you could hire someone who is fluent in the language and culture of the reader, in this case the United States, to write the letter for you. The person can collect information about the recommender and your professional interactions and then put that in a recommendation letter that uses the words and the structure expected of such a letter in the United States. If the person that writes the letter is also familiar with your language and culture, even better. To continue with our example, such a person would know the meaning of "Adjunct Professor" in your country and would use the proper terminology in American English, thus making sure that your recommender is represented correctly in the language of those who will read your application materials.

Before we continue, a gentle reminder: These documents are written for readers who have a lot to do and not very much time. Therefore, just like with resumes, letters of recommendation should be strategic about the use of space. They should be just one to two pages long, at most. This means that what is said and how it is said should be decided with care. The length of a letter matters so much for some institutions that they will sometimes publish a limit on the number of characters (and spaces) accepted. Anything above that limit will be cut off when you upload such a letter, meaning disregarding the limit will only hurt you.

Now to the requirements of a letter of recommendation, from the first to the last line.

At the top of the letter, we have the recommender's name and contact information. An email and phone number are required, and an address is usual, but not essential. (Recommenders never get contacted by mail, so this information is increasingly obsolete.)

However, if your recommender is based in the U.S., an American address can be valuable, as it indicates that your recommender is (supposedly) acquainted with the way things work in the U.S. This perception may add credibility to what the recommender writes about you in the text that follows.

After the name and contact information comes the date and greeting. Remember that Americans use the month before the day of the month (August 13, 2013, for example) and that you are allowed to call anybody "Dear," no matter how high their position (as in "Dear President").

The first portion of the actual letter text should be a simple phrase about how excited/enthusiastic/delighted the recommender is for the opportunity to recommend such a great person as you. If the recommender has known you for a long time, the beginning might mention the number of years. This is because longevity can invite confidence in what the recommender has to say.

Next comes a paragraph describing the credentials of the recommender. Since space is limited, emphasize the highlights of the recommender's career without going into detail.

This section can include education, work experience, leadership positions, etc. Here it is difficult to give specific advice, given that what constitutes "strong credentials" varies from field to field. For example, if your recommender was your professor, their academic credentials should stand out. If they were your supervisor at a company, their professional experiences at companies of renown would matter more.

Next comes the section about you. I suggest the following sequence, with the understanding that each person's trajectory is unique and not everything will apply in your case.

When did you first meet and under what circumstances? Be as specific as possible to create an image in the mind of the reader.

What was your relationship when you met (employee-supervisor, student-professor, colleagues)?

If you were engaged professionally over a longer period, did your relationship change? If yes, how? (For example, perhaps you started as student and professor and later became colleagues at the same educational institution or company.)

Describe concrete examples of your work together. If you worked together over a long time, are there examples of growth in the candidate that can be described through indicators such as an increase in productivity or an increase in responsibility?

If you have many examples of projects you did together, use a paragraph for each, truly giving the reader a variety of examples that offer evidence of a range of qualities. This may also be a good place for the recommender to share how their impressions of you changed over time (always for the better, of course).

Ideally, the recommender should be aware of the position you are seeking and include specific references to how they believe you can contribute to the company, educational institution, or the country.

The final part of the letter should briefly summarize what was said in the core paragraphs and reiterate that the recommender believes that you are a perfect match for the position in question. The recommender can also mention that they are available to be contacted in case there are questions about the letter or about you.

This completes the letter!

P.S.: Don't forget to tell your recommender about the outcome of your application. People want to feel that they are part of your dream, whether the letter's outcome was positive or not. Not talking with your recommender after you received a reply to your application can appear like you don't care about their participation in your dream and that only contacted them because you wanted something from them.

13

INTERVIEWS

If you are reading this, chances are that you got an interview invitation and need to prepare. Before you do anything else, send a thank you note to the person who sent you the invite and say you are looking forward to it—even if you are scared out of your mind. And do it immediately, not tomorrow, because that is what is expected.

Since thank you notes are so important, I will add this now, rather than at the end of this chapter: You are also expected to write a thank you note after the interview. This thank you note can be just a "thank you for your time" type of text, but ideally it would mention something about the interview that enhances the perception that you are a great fit for the opportunity. This reminder can help jog the interviewer's memory, particularly if many people were interviewed on the same day.

Now let's look at the interview itself.

Interviews, like cover letters and statements of intent, are opportunities to prove that you would be the right fit for a university, an organization, or the country. To prove that you are the right fit, you must do two things: first, know what they are looking for, and second, present evidence that you are the right person to fulfill their needs. Let's break that down a bit more.

1. Know them and what they are looking for. Too often I see clients who believe they are strong candidates because they work hard and/or because they are passionate about what they do. True, being hardworking and passionate are all good things in a candidate. However, that alone won't get you in the door.

Remember that the opportunity that you want only came about because the university, the company, or the country, has a need. Unless you clearly demonstrate that you are the right person to fill their needs, your hard work and passion mean nothing to the person assessing your application. In other words, you are here for them, and not the other way around.

And to be here for them, you have to do a great deal of research to know who they are, what they want, and why. Only then will you be able to talk convincingly about why you are the best person to give them what they need.

How do you do such research? First, thoroughly study the official site of the organization you are hoping to join. Follow every link available so you can dig as deep as they will let you. Also look for information about the organization in news available on sites that don't speak for the organization. What are independent newspapers saying? What are third-party reports revealing? As usual, make sure to get your information about the organization from reputable sources. Some sources are suggested below.

For university programs, search information about faculty and their publications, program curriculum, available research centers, and other indicators of what the university's focus and resources are. If the university has many programs that could be a good fit for you, study their differences and be able to explain your choice, should you be asked in an interview why you selected A over B.

For jobs, search information about the company and about current and former employees on sites such as LinkedIn. It is especially informative to read about the work experience of people you may join as colleagues or people you might be replacing. (In situations such as the latter, if you have a way to learn about the reasons the person is leaving, even better.)

For immigration visas, if you are in charge of writing your own Professional Plan—or any other document that explains why you are poised to make tremendous contributions to the country—seek data about your field, including projected growth, on sites like the United States Bureau of Labor Statistics (www.bls.gov) and sites that produce market reports.

2. Present evidence that shows why you are the one. For any claim, Americans expect to see supporting data. (See chapter "Evidence.") Any person interviewing for an opportunity can claim that they are a perfect fit, but it is the candidate who can back that claim with data that will be noticed. It is the candidate who can demonstrate fit with concrete examples rather than vague statements that will win the race.

Evidence of fit can be shown in many ways. Let's look at two examples:

Let's say you are applying for a post-graduate program at a university. Let's also imagine that you conducted research on a specific topic in your country, and there is a professor in the program you wish to join who conducts research on the same topic. In a potential interview, you should bring up the match between your research interests and that of the professor. This shows that you are a natural fit for that professor.

This professor may also be interested in expanding their research and doing a comparative study between countries, in which case your research in your country could serve the professor. And, you bring experience in this particular area, which means the professor wouldn't have to spend as much time training you as they would have to spend on a novice. Do you see how your past can serve as evidence that you are the best candidate?

Maybe you are applying for a job where your main task would be to solve a series of technical problems. As you prepare for the interview, conduct research about how this company has tried to solve these problems before. What solutions have been attempted without yielding the desired results? Your application should focus on how your experience with similar challenges has prepared you to solve these technical problems once and for all.

After you have done your research about the organization you want to join and have defined how you can contribute, you will be ready to engage in an exercise that can feel annoying but is key to acing an interview. Remember that Americans value preparedness (see chapter "Time"), and this exercise is the best way to prepare.

Sit down and write a list of questions you might be asked. Search "interview questions" online and you will find plenty of examples. Then select and write down a few questions that are more likely to be asked for the type of position you are applying for. There is no need to reproduce the questions here because the possibilities are so many and easy to access online. (I do offer tips below about how to prepare for five questions that are common yet can be tricky to answer.)

Once you have chosen a list of 15-20 questions you think are most applicable to your situation, proceed to answer each question in your own words, perhaps using bullet points, essentially figuring out what you want to make sure to say if you were asked that question in an interview. At the end of this exercise, you should have a few pages of information that summarize key points about your career and how you can contribute to this organization. Next, you want to practice answering these questions with a friend, or in front of a mirror.

You may feel that you are wasting your time answering hypothetical questions. Two reasons make this exercise essential and not a waste.

First, with this exercise, you will have all the information you want to convey to your interviewer(s) in one place. Even if the interview questions you get asked are not the same questions you prepared, they will be related. Your preparation will allow you to quickly retrieve related information from your memory and rephrase as needed. This preparedness will likely be noticed by your interviewer and count in your favor.

The second reason to spend time preparing in this way is that when you do this exercise, you automatically gain confidence. You enter the interview calmer, you walk a little taller, and your handshake is firmer. Confidence is a priceless asset that never fails to impress, and that alone is a good reason to spend time building it up prior to an interview.

Let's look at five questions that can be a bit tricky, especially for international candidates.

1. Tell us a bit about yourself. This question is deceptively simple and purposely vague. Interviewers like this question because its openness allows the candidate to take the answer in any direction they like. And interviewers will be watching carefully where you take it. Will you talk about your spouse, your kids, and how much you all want to move to the U.S.? (Wrong answer.) Will you talk only about what you did in the past? (No.) Will you tell them only about why you love their program? (Incomplete.)

The answer should not be a complete summary of your past accomplishments and your dreams for the future. Instead, it is a chance to tell them about only three to four things you want them to remember about you. That number is about all their brains will recall after you leave. So be intentional when you decide what is most important they remember about you. Decide how you could speak about these few things in a manner that is interesting and supported by memorable examples. (People tend to remember concrete examples more than abstract concepts.)

2. Tell us about why you believe you are a good fit for our company/program. This question is obviously a chance for you to tell interviewers about the reasons you and the company/program are a match. What you may not realize is that this question is also a way for them to check what you know about them! If you tell interviewers for a university program that you think you are a good fit because you want to do research, but their program materials say nothing about research, you just got your application in the "not a good fit" pile.

3. Tell us about your strengths. This question can be tricky because you need to speak highly of your skills but also do so with humility. Let's have some fun with what unabashed self-promotion might look like: "I'm the best candidate you have ever come across. I'm an excellent problem solver, an extraordinary manager, and a remarkable team player."

Instead of these vague self-promoting statements that anybody could make, present concrete examples that show the same qualities. Examples speak for themselves, allowing you to impress without having to announce it from the rooftops.

4. Tell us about your weaknesses. In an interview, you are supposed to look strong, right? So, what is a question about weakness doing here? This question can sound like the interviewer is trying to trick you. But if you are prepared to answer it, this question is an opportunity for you to look quite good, actually.

You are going to mention a weakness in response. After all, you don't want to sound like you didn't understand the question or don't like to follow instructions. However, your example should come from the past! Your example should tell a story about a weakness you had in the past and how you realized that this weakness was hindering your ability to be more X or Y. (X or Y are things that are valued in your field.)

Then you should proceed to tell the interviewer how you have dealt with the weakness and how this struggle has helped you improve as a person and professional. You should also state how you have continued to work on this (mostly former) weakness because you know habits are hard to break and you see each day as an opportunity to continue improving.

By presenting your weakness in this manner, you tell them several positive things:

a. You can see when a behavior is hindering your success. (You just showed self-awareness, which is highly valued by Americans.)

b. You are able to see a problem, come up with a strategy to fix it, and implement the strategy. (Priceless, especially if you are applying to a position that requires problem-solving.)

c. You recognize that big problems require long-term solutions, and you are putting this knowledge into practice in your own daily life.

5. What questions do you have for us? By the time this question arises at the end of the interview, you will be mentally drained and tempted to say, "No questions, thank you so much." Such an answer deflates the interviewer for two reasons. First, it takes away a chance for them to talk about their program and themselves. Remember that your interviewer is a human being, and people generally like to talk about themselves and be listened to. When you don't have any questions, you deprive them of such an opportunity.

Second, by having no questions (or worse, by asking questions that are well explained on their website or were already answered) you are effectively saying that you didn't do your homework. You didn't study their information, and you didn't consider your qualifications in light of what you learned in your research.

This question should be used, instead, to demonstrate that you read all their materials (you are curious and a good learner) and that you took that information and went further with it (you can expand on what is given to you and think about it in new ways). A simple example: "While going over the materials you have available on your site, I noticed X. This made me curious about how your company applies X to situations where Y is present. In the work I do currently, we often have Y present and I have learned that…" You just took the question and turned it into a statement that shows you studied their material, are curious about what you found, and have had some similar experiences that could be useful to them.

There is something important you should know about this last question and the interview overall: When they ask if you have questions, it may be tempting to ask practical questions such as salary and benefits. If they have not offered this information, this is <u>not</u> the time to ask about it. Why? Because your focus at this stage of the game should be on the match between you and the opportunity. These other— yes, very important—questions are best presented after your interviewer is convinced that they can't do without you. Then you will be in a much stronger position to negotiate.

As the interview comes to a close, it is also appropriate to ask your interviewer about their timeline. For example, you may ask, "What are the next steps in your search process?" or "When do you expect to make a decision?" Make note of the date they mention and if you have not heard back from them by then, it is totally acceptable to send a quick email stating that you are looking forward to hearing from them when they have made their decision.

Remember to also send that thank you email I mentioned earlier. Though some interviewers will state that they don't care if they get a thank you, I have heard others say that they will not offer a position to a candidate who fails to attend to something so simple. It is best to just do it, and within a few hours of the completion of the interview.

Other than that, good luck! Because luck is a factor in how an interview goes, too! Don't take all the credit, but also don't take all the blame for whatever happens between you and the interviewer. It is a dance, and you are only one of the partners.

14
ELEVATOR PITCH

In the United States, cultivating a circle of professional contacts who may be helpful to your career development in the future is key to success.[19] This continuous cultivation of professional contacts is called networking and has an almost godly reputation for solving just about any career problem. For example, if a person can't find a job, the most common explanation will be that they are not networking right or hard enough. While this may be true, it is also likely that other factors are at play, such as a recession or a pandemic. But this faith in networking is in keeping with the American belief that individual hard work and an indomitable drive to succeed are the answers to life's challenges.

Continuously attracting new contacts and greasing the wheels of those relationships long-term can happen in many ways. For example, the people that you study with and work with are part of your network. When you graduate or change jobs, your old contacts, if you remain in touch at least occasionally, will continue to be a part of your network. Moreover, any person you already know can help you meet

19 You can find plenty of data online supporting this claim, but just to give you one example, a CNBC article from February 2020 reports that "as much as 80% of jobs are filled through personal and professional connections."

new people—www.linkedin.com is a great tool for this—and those new people then become part of your network.

In academia, conferences are an important venue to reconnect with old professors and colleagues every few years. These events are where you will hear about what your contacts are doing and tell them about what you are up to. You may even leave the conference with an invitation to apply for a job, co-author a journal article, or present at a panel organized by a former colleague. For professionals outside of academia, there are annual gatherings such as trade shows where you will meet some of the same people again and again and have conversations that could result in new opportunities or new partnerships. See why networking has almost magical properties?

You can find many resources online to teach you how to network, so I won't repeat them here. But what may not be clear to international professionals such as yourself is that you can prepare ahead of time for these networking opportunities. You can prepare an elevator pitch (or elevator speech), which you can bring out anytime you find yourself in a situation that may result in a new contact. This mini speech is called an elevator pitch in reference to the brief moment we meet strangers while riding in an elevator together.

Now that you know the importance of the elevator pitch, let's answer a few simple questions about it.

What is an Elevator Pitch?
A brief summary about your professional trajectory to be shared with people who don't know you yet but could become important contributors to your career development in the future.

How short?

Short enough that it could be delivered while you and the other person are riding in an elevator together from one floor to another. Short enough that it can sound like a casual conversation, though you prepared and rehearsed it ahead of time.

Where can I use it?

Anywhere you can create an opportunity to introduce yourself (or reintroduce yourself). This includes in-person and virtual meetings, trainings, professional events, and more low-key settings such as an airport lounge, hotel waiting area, or coffee shop line. The opportunities are endless, as long as you are a good people-reader and understand when people want to hear more and when they just want to be left alone.

How do I create an elevator pitch?

Begin by inspecting your resume and updating any portion that may be outdated. (After all, a good elevator pitch could lead to a request for your resume on the spot!) When you look at the entirety of your professional history, what stands out? What is most memorable and reflects your expertise? What are you most proud of and would want potential bosses or colleagues to know about you?

If this sounds like self-branding, it is because it is! You want to present the best you've got in the little time you have.

As in self-branding, you want to consider who your audience is. For example, if you are an engineer, and you are talking to a lay person, it may be enough to say, "I am an engineer." But if you are talking to another engineer, you may want to be more specific. A phrase such as "I am a civil engineer specializing in suspension bridges" says much more to this listener than if you simply described yourself as an engineer. Remember: How you present yourself is always determined by who your audience is.

Depending on your field, it may also be important to describe who you serve and how. Who are your clients? How do you make their lives better? What is the purpose of what you offer and why does it matter? In my case, my elevator pitch may say that I help international professionals be understood and valued in the United States so that their dreams in this country can become reality. Someone who designs wheelchairs makes life better by helping people with their mobility. If this person wanted to be more specific, they could say they develop new wheelchair designs to address old accessibility problems for which there had been no solutions until now.

It is less important to provide an exact description of what you do than it is to offer a bit of information that piques the listener's interest and gets them to ask a follow-up question. That keeps the conversation going, and interesting conversations are where potential future opportunities come from.

The potential "ask"

If the person you are having this brief exchange with is in the same field as you, you can include what Americans call an "ask." For example, if you are looking for a new job, you can say that you are "exploring new opportunities," "making a career change," or "hoping to contribute to a company that does X."

How to end it

If the exchange is going well and there seems to be a mutual interest in continuing the conversation, let the other person know how they can reach you and ask how you can reach them. A follow-up, especially if there were asks involved in your original conversation, is expected, and will not be seen as annoying.

How you end depends entirely on where you want to take this connection, if anywhere. This person may have no understanding of the professional value you bring to others. With such a person, the conversation can end right there with, "It was so nice to meet you. Take care."

However, sometimes even a person who has nothing in common with you may be curious about what you do and want to learn more. That person may be worth adding to your professional network because of the people they know. If they are enthusiastic about what they heard from you, they might mention you and what you do to some-body else, who may be just the kind of connection you were looking for.

Elevator pitches are a low-key way to meet people, yet they could have an enormous impact on your future. You have nothing to lose by preparing an elevator pitch, and everything to gain if you are suddenly in the right place, at the right time, with the right people. That is what Americans would call "grabbing life by the horns."

Now that you know what to do, let's get to it!

ACKNOWLEDGMENTS

Without my parents, Heide and Nelson Kirst, there would be no life in the United States to write about. In their parental brilliance, they advised me, an aspiring theater director, to take a once-in-a-lifetime opportunity to travel to the U.S. and polish my English. This way, if my future theater career didn't pay the bills, I could always teach English on the side. What wisdom! Plan B became my Plan A and brought me a life of rich opportunities to learn about cultures and become the bridge between people and countries that I was meant to be.

But getting to a new country isn't enough. One must remain long enough to really learn. I would never have remained in the U.S. had it not been for the kind support of Anna Mae Patterson, to whom this book is dedicated. Anna Mae, your home, your guidance, and your generosity are the reasons I stayed and eventually learned that the United States was more complex than my stereotypes. Without you, I also would not have met Mark Schultz, and there would be no Sen and Bela!

Thank you to my children, Sen and Bela, who grew up in the United States yet never had the easy relationship with their country that is a given for those who grow up without much awareness of the world beyond American borders. I gave you more than your fair share to deconstruct about the country that is your home!

Thank you to all of those who made me an anthropologist, including my first professor of anthropology at UFRGS, Dr. Ondina Fachel Leal, and my mentors, Dr. Mike

Nakkula, then from the Harvard Graduate School, and Dr. Sarah Lamb, from Brandeis University. I would not be the professional, the educator, and the writer I have become without your guidance and modeling.

Thank you to all the international students and professionals who taught me so much about what it means to be from elsewhere and set roots in a country that is not always easy to understand. Some of you even read early chapters and shared your impressions. Among them were Leonardo Araujo, Vinicius Carvalho, Luciana Flores, Ausubel Pichardo, Luisi Silva, and Gustavo Viola. Thank you!

Thank you to the members of the writing group "Writing is Better Together" who have provided the company that makes for consistent writing. I am especially indebted to Jenna MacIntire and Gene Christy, who made us become a group when I was about to give up.

Thank you to Jennifer Browdy, Professor of Comparative Literature and Media Arts at Bard College at Simon's Rock, for encouraging me to think of this book as a resource for international students in colleges and universities in the United States. It is thrilling to return to this work, just from outside this time.

Dani Senger read the final manuscript with a degree of attention that only a dedicated friend, colleague, and language expert could do. When I got tired, she reminded me that what is in these pages is valuable and can help dreams come true.

Each of you, in your own way, made this book possible.

With gratitude,
Júlia

ABOUT THE AUTHOR

Júlia Kirst, Ph.D., is a Brazilian-American cultural anthropologist living between countries and cultures since birth. In the U.S. permanently since 1997, she holds a master's degree from Harvard University and a doctorate from Brandeis University. After a career teaching international students about the United States in American colleges and universities, she turned to the development of a business dedicated to helping international professionals be understood and valued in the United States. With expertise in cross-cultural communication, anthropology, psychology, and marketing, she offers cross-cultural strategy, writing, and trainings for international applicants who have a dream to fulfill in the United States. You can find out more about Dr. Kirst and her work at www.juliakirst.com.

www.ingramcontent.com/pod-product-compliance
Lightning Source LLC
Chambersburg PA
CBHW070117030426
42335CB00016B/2182